Embracing the Exceptions

Neurodivergent students of color are often overlooked, as research and teaching strategies predominantly focus on white males in the classroom. How can we help teachers reach all students to honor their full humanity, and to understand how ableism – neuronormativity in particular – and racism intersect on our bodies and brains? JPB Gerald's fascinating book offers a blend of narrative and interviews to show what would help neurodivergent students of color feel more supported and cared for in schools, and to demonstrate how much better their lives could be when they feel that love. Each chapter covers a common trait among neurodivergent students, and concludes with takeaways and approaches for supporting our youth in the classroom. Turning from a deficit-based look to a strength-based one, JPB helps us see how NDSOC students think and learn differently, and how we can do right by them, supporting them more effectively in the classroom and beyond.

JPB Gerald is an adult educator and theorist, and a 2022 graduate of the EdD program in Instructional Leadership from CUNY – Hunter College, USA. Through his writing, teaching, podcast and his public scholarship overall, he seeks justice for the racially, linguistically and neurologically minoritized.

Equity and Social Justice in Education Series

Paul C. Gorski, Series Editor

Routledge's Equity and Social Justice in Education series is a publishing home for books that apply critical and transformative equity and social justice theories to the work of on-the-ground educators. Books in the series describe meaningful solutions to the racism, white supremacy, economic injustice, sexism, heterosexism, transphobia, ableism, neoliberalism, and other oppressive conditions that pervade schools and school districts.

Equity-Centered Trauma-Informed Education
Alex Shevrin Venet

Learning and Teaching While White: Antiracist Strategies for School Communities
Jenna Chandler-Ward and Elizabeth Denevi

Public School Equity: Educational Leadership for Justice
Manya C. Whitaker

Ableism in Education: Rethinking School Practices and Policies
Gillian Parekh

Becoming an Everyday Changemaker: Healing and Justice At School
Alex Shevrin Venet

Embracing the Exceptions: Meeting the Needs of Neurodivergent Students of Color
JPB Gerald

Embracing the Exceptions

Meeting the Needs of Neurodivergent Students of Color

JPB Gerald

Routledge
Taylor & Francis Group

NEW YORK AND LONDON

Designed cover image: © Getty Images

First published 2025
by Routledge
605 Third Avenue, New York, NY 10158

and by Routledge
4 Park Square, Milton Park, Abingdon, Oxon, OX14 4RN

Routledge is an imprint of the Taylor & Francis Group, an informa business

Library of Congress Cataloging-in-Publication Data
Names: Gerald, J. P. B. , 1986– author.
Title: Embracing the exceptions : meeting the needs of neurodivergent
    students of color / JPB Gerald.
Description: New York, NY : Routledge, 2024. | Series: Equity and
    social justice in education | Includes bibliographical references.
Identifiers: LCCN 2024014263 (print) | LCCN 2024014264 (ebook) |
    ISBN 9781032729961 (paperback) | ISBN 9781003465126 (ebook)
Subjects: LCSH: Neurodivergent children—Education. |
    Neurodivergent youth—Education. | Children of minorities—
    Education. | Minority youth—Education.
Classification: LCC LC4717 .G47 2024 (print) | LCC LC4717 (ebook) |
    DDC 371.829—dc23/eng/20240522
LC record available at https://lccn.loc.gov/2024014263
LC ebook record available at https://lccn.loc.gov/2024014264

ISBN: 978-1-032-72996-1 (pbk)
ISBN: 978-1-003-46512-6 (ebk)

DOI: 10.4324/9781003465126

Typeset in Palatino
by Apex CoVantage, LLC

Contents

Prologue

I might have far too many letters after my name, but, even though I still do it occasionally, I don't particularly enjoy writing for a purely academic audience. My first book – an academic examination of white supremacy in the language teaching industry – was well-received, but it has a necessarily limited reach, and, frankly, I'm not sure anyone actually listens to academics when they're not on a university campus, because most of us don't particularly know how to talk to anyone whose name doesn't start with "Dr."

I say this because, much as I am proud of my scholarly achievements, I remain concerned that these ideas will not, as an out-of-touch economist might say, trickle down to folks who are actually on the ground supporting young learners on a daily basis. On top of that, when I think about my own experiences and what would have helped me, it would have been teachers being given the opportunity to listen to communities they hadn't been trained to consider, particularly at intersections of identity that aren't well-covered by readily available research.

Like a lot of people who are eventually diagnosed with ADHD, I obviously always had it, but, also like a lot of us, I was never evaluated until Something Went Wrong. For many, this is a struggle with testing in school, but the particular manifestation of my own manner of thinking made it pretty easy for me to memorize enough to excel on standardized tests, and in fact to complete them very quickly – you'll hear a lot more about this later in the book. For me, though, I finally ran into a wall I couldn't just put my head down and barrel through when I was struggling at work and almost lost my job because I kept making minor errors while editing documents during the early stages of the COVID-19 pandemic. I will describe my full evaluation and diagnosis process throughout the book, but for now I will say that I was filled with two primary emotions when they finally told me what I'd, by then, strongly suspected for several years: relief and sadness. Relief, because I had confirmation that there actually wasn't anything "wrong" with me. As the interviews you will later read excerpts from will make clear, the toxic shame that often accompanies neurodivergence is possibly the most difficult feature of our identities, and, no matter how many years of treatment we may receive, it's incredibly hard to shake once and for all. Who knows if I ever truly will?

But mostly, at that moment, I felt sadness. I was sad because the evaluator told me that I'd developed exceptional "compensation mechanisms," as she called them, or ways to move through the world, suppressing the divergence to try and connect with my peers and succeed in school, work, and life, and it sure did seem like I could have saved myself a lot of time and stress had I only been supported instead of mostly dismissed as somewhat annoying. I thought about all the work I had done to feel less isolated and how, until I finally got this information, it had only been marginally effective. I reflected, mostly, on my years in school, particularly from second grade to 12th, when I was always loved and supported by my family but left to fend for myself in class because they saw me, a Black boy who was "smart" enough to be accepted into an exclusive institution, as someone who didn't need (or deserve?) any help. Indeed, though there is thankfully a growing body of discourse around supporting *white* neurodivergent students, I still don't see myself or the other people you'll meet in this book in much of the literature.

The people you'll meet in this book are adults, and are reflecting on their time as neurodivergent students of color. Because of the direction my own life has taken and the fact that I found them through my own networks, a lot of them have advanced degrees and are, by all standardized metrics, successful. This is certainly a limitation to the scope of the narratives you'll read, but I don't see much value in using extreme trauma to get people to care – my assumption in writing this book is that you already care and simply need more detail on our particular ways of being. Our traumatic experiences will still come up, because the world, and the education system, isn't really built to support us, but you are ultimately reading about people who "won" the battle.

With that said, I resist the urge to refer to our neurodivergence as some sort of "superpower," because, for many if not all of us, it can truly be an impediment to success or even stability. I will cite more specific statistics later, but a disproportionate percentage of the incarcerated population is suspected of being neurodivergent – ADHD in particular – and I don't think anyone reading this would be unaware of how disproportionately non-white this same population is. Now, I say "suspected" for a reason – the reason this book is necessary is because we simply do not look like what people are taught to expect from neurodivergence, and we are also woefully underdiagnosed.[1] To be exceptionally clear, there is no biological difference between races, but the ways we are socialized – or, really, allowed – to behave in public are shaped by stereotypes and fears and expectations that we all are forced to live under. Our brains are fundamentally the same as those of white neurodivergent students, but we are seen, and, unfortunately, treated differently, and that treatment, and our reaction to it, our methods for achieving regardless of our obstacles, is what you are going to hear from us in these pages.

I should also say, before we get into the body of all this, that I feel an immense responsibility in bringing these stories to the public. Though I may cite a few examples that are buried deep inside inaccessible academic journals, people haven't heard from us as a community before, and certainly not in a way that could help teachers support us more effectively. Indeed, the teacher part of this is key – every single one of us was supported by one or more teachers who truly saw us, whether or not they knew of our neurodivergent status. I myself wasn't diagnosed until I was 35, but I still had a few teachers who understood why I did things the way I did them, and without them I wouldn't have gotten anywhere close to where I've ended up. I want you, teachers reading this, to be able to play that role for students who are like the kid I once was, who are like the others you'll meet in this book, even if their neurodivergence looks different from what you've been taught to take note of, and even if you don't know for sure that they're neurodivergent. For all the challenges you'll hear about later, I write this because I think that, if you want to be that teacher, all you have to do is take a bit of extra time and understand the way we move through the world, and the ways that might differ from the neurodivergent stereotype of a white boy who struggles on exams and just can't sit still.

To that point, this book is not at all meant to discourage teachers from supporting the neurodivergent students who fit the expected behavior patterns. Indeed, all we need is the patience and care that those students are already provided. You'll hear of much worse – even just in my own story, you'll hear of teachers singling me out in front of the class for forgetfulness and dis-organization – but I choose to trust that you wouldn't do what those teachers did, and are searching for tools to reach what is ultimately a giant population of students whose voices have yet to be heard. The numbers are fuzzy, but if the non-white popula-tion of the country is just over 40% (and on the relative increase),[2] and 15–20% of the overall population is neurodivergent,[3] then we're talking about 6–8% of the United States population that could be classified as a neurodivergent person of color – more than 20 million people as of this writing. There are far too many of us not to have a book about us, for us, and by (one of) us, and I only hope I can do us justice.

And so, I am writing this book for the boy I once was, so that all the others like him don't have to spend decades trying to work out what's "wrong" with them because their teachers and schools are happy to let us flail. I'm not in a place to give advice to parents given my handful of years as a father so far, but I am an educator, and I do have relevant expertise on issues of both racism and ableism, so I hope that what I share with any teachers who read this book can help the kids like us that they happen to find in their classrooms feel the psychological safety and support that many of us once lacked.

This, as I hinted above, will absolutely not be a solemn, mournful book about being a kid with social struggles, espe-cially because I don't want to make my parents too upset. No, there will be plenty of joy in these pages, and plenty of the particular brilliance that can only be found in our community when we're given the tools to thrive. So read on, educators, if you are interested in building your knowledge base and improving your strategies for embracing the exceptions you've been tasked with teaching.

Ultimately, I can't go back in time to help the kid I once was, but in some way, I think he might thank me anyway.

Notes

1   Aylward, B.S., Gal-Szabo, D.E., and Taraman, S. (2021) Racial, Ethnic, and Sociodemographic Disparities in Diagnosis of Children with Autism Spectrum Disorder. *Journal of Developmental & Behavioral Pediatrics* 42 (8), 682–689. doi:10.1097/DBP.0000000000000996. PMID: 34510108; PMCID: PMC8500365.
2   https://www.census.gov/quickfacts/fact/table/US/PST045222
3   https://www.ncbi.nlm.nih.gov/pmc/articles/PMC7732033/

Introduction

Bio

I'm a cishet man born and raised on unceded Munsee Lenape territory, which you'd know better as NYC. I'm Black, and even though my great-grandmother was Cherokee, I know very little about that aspect of my background so it feels disingenuous to claim it or put it down on any official forms. I'm also, apparently, one-sixteenth Irish, according to some research I've done.

I went to a private school in Brooklyn for 14 years (1989–2003), a school I won't name but suffice it to say I was in class with future celebrities like Lena Dunham and Jemima Kirke – *if you've never seen HBO's "Girls," I envy you* – which was, uh, interesting. We'll get back to that. I went to an Ivy League school for undergrad, was an English major and kind of a middling student with very few extracurriculars and not a lot of confidence, and then I graduated without any sort of career plan, which is all well and good except it also meant I didn't have a job. I found out that they hired just about any American college graduate to teach English overseas – still true! – and I ended up in Daegu, South Korea, when I was still just 21. (*I skipped first grade – yes, we'll get into that too.*) I was entirely unqualified to teach the high schoolers I was tasked with, which is something we subject far too many learners to, but, by my second year, I was actually pretty good at connecting with my students, and I decided to make a go of it as a career, so I came home to get a Master's and actually know more than nothing about pedagogy.

Because I wasn't state-certified, I picked up odd teaching jobs during my degree, and the only places I could get (contingent, poorly paid, uninsured) work was at schools that taught either exchange students or newly arrived immigrants, another group upon which we foist people who aren't as credentialed. In 2012, after graduating with my MA, I got a more stable – but still

DOI: 10.4324/9781003465126-1

poorly paid – job running an adult education program at a settlement house in Manhattan, where I was responsible for assessing, enrolling, evaluating, and teaching the students, alongside a bevy of very friendly but often completely inexperienced volunteers. During this tenure, I met my now-wife, who convinced me I was undervalued, and I made what was at the time a difficult decision to leave the full-time classroom after nine years and move more into curriculum development.

We can mostly skip the next job except to note that because the role was affiliated with CUNY (the City University of New York), I got a slight discount on their associated schools and I applied to and was accepted into the EdD program in Instructional Leadership at Hunter College. I went to school part-time while keeping my job, a job that eventually started to go south and which I managed to barely hold onto, a large reason for why I finally got evaluated and diagnosed with ADHD in late 2021. As I finally neared both the publication of my first (academic) book and my graduation, I got my current (as of this writing) job, leading the curriculum development and instruction for a large national program that trains housing developers of color to stem the tide of gentrification and predatory development. I am no real estate expert, but after what is now 16 years in education, 12 years in adult education, and seven years in curriculum development, I feel like I can say I know pedagogy. I also adjunct in an education department for fun, because I do love teaching and I missed it, and so I remain involved in teaching teachers, even if it's not my main gig. And I write essays, articles, and books. So here we are.

ND + POC

In order for this book to work, it's important I be extremely clear about the language I will be using. Indeed, part of the issue with these topics is that we aren't always able to determine what we mean when we say things like "neurodivergent," "people (or students) of color," and, to speak more broadly, "disability" and "race."

Let's get this straight from the jump, then – "race" is not a biological fact. Despite what some folks might try to tell you, there is nothing innately different, scientifically, between people seen as Black and white (*my capitalization – or lack thereof – is for political reasons you can read about throughout this section*), or South Asian, or Pacific Islander, or anything else. Sure, you can take a genetic test or do public records research to determine your ancestry, which is a different but related concept, but who your great-grandparents were doesn't have a whole lot to do with how you, today, are seen in the city, state, and country in which you live. Race, as we know it today, is something we – well, *they* – made up to justify *racism*, and it is not a tangible reality. Yet with all of that said, just because it was constructed – and is constantly shifting and narrowing and expanding – does not mean it isn't real, because it does have a tangible impact on all of us, whether or not we would like it to, and whether or not we would like to admit it. I would hope we are past the time when people could profess not to "see color," as that sort of color-evasiveness is ultimately more harmful than helpful. Indeed, if you are reading this book, you are trying to do your best to look directly at students of color, as we are often left out of the neurodivergent story.

Another reason I am being explicit that I am writing about race rather than culture or something even vaguer like "background" is because it remains a topic that is uncomfortable for many to sit with. Even when we try to be inclusive and speak of, say, cultural sensitivity or cultural competence in the classroom, people still choose to avoid considering race in these efforts. Years ago, I started focusing my writing on race because I asked some fellow language teachers if they ever talked about race in their classrooms, and even some of the people who said "yes" actually said they were happy to discuss their students' "cultures," which is not the same thing. Cultures, of course, are also constructed and constantly evolving, but we need to really focus on the issue at hand if we are to support the students in question.

Now, despite my using "of color" here and throughout the book, skin tone is really only the surface of the issue, that pun being fully intended. I am using that phrasing mostly for convenience and readability, but if I were going deep into academic theory I would be more likely to use the term *minoritized*, or, even better *racialized as* (insert race). Race is contextual, see; for someone like me or the others you will meet in this book, we will be classified differently depending on where we are or what we are doing. The list of racial categories I've been placed into when traveling to different places is comically long, though there was always a subtle theme of belonging to an underclass familiar to a particular context. For example, here in the States, they definitely accurately peg me as specifically African-American, but in France, they assume I'm actually from the continent of Africa, which makes sense if you think about colonial history. When living in South Korea, I was sometimes mistaken for Filipino, which is pretty funny if you've ever seen me before, but there are a fair amount of migrant workers from the Philippines in that country, and so I think you can start to understand the point I am making. Amusingly, after the presidential election of 2008, the South Koreans I encountered suddenly "got" that I was Black because there was a rather famous Black person on TV all the time they could associate me with.

On our outdated census forms, African-Americans and Africans are usually mushed together, and Filipinos are thrown into an absurdly geographically wide region referred to as "Pacific Islands." I can choose to *identify* however I want to, but how I feel about myself often has very little to do with how I am seen within my surroundings, and we are all *racialized* by forces out of our control. I could even identify as white if I felt so inclined, but it wouldn't do a whole lot for me if I got pulled over on the highway, which is why I strongly prefer not to drive if I can help it.

Minoritized works similarly – the "-ize" shows that it's a process that has little to do with how numerous a group is. We all understand that small numbers of people can wield outsize power, and that how much power a group has is essentially unrelated to whether or not they comprise a numerical majority. The richest people in the world are certainly a very small *minority*, but they are by no means minorit*ized*, if you catch my drift. Nevertheless, for the purposes of this book, I will mostly be using *people/students of color* – even though it's not really about "color" – so I don't have to bore you by overexplaining more esoteric terminology. I do encourage everyone reading this to understand the intertwined processes of racialization and minoritization, and to understand how archaic the term *minority* is when referring to the people in this book.

Now, who gets to be included or excluded from the category of "white" is a dense, complex question I spend time analyzing in my academic work which you can read if you'd like to. The short version is that there is no one definition, at least not one that doesn't need constant revision. The answer to the question, "Can (group) be white?" is almost always, "It depends." Groups that can be said to have ceased being classified as people of color include the Irish, Germans, Italians, Finns, and many other European countries,[1] however, in every single example above, the qualifier "most" needs to be added, because there are always exceptions. The racial covenants in housing deeds that helped ensure racial homogeneity in many American towns and suburbs[2] were often very clear about who was allowed to buy certain houses, but that list differed from location to location. There are of course also many people who have "passed" for white because of their appearance, which is a rare example of people who may have identified as Black while being racialized as white. My point is, there is no single answer to this question, and I make no attempt to provide one. However, what is absolutely true is that, regardless of my and my interviewees' skin tone or ancestry, we were all seen as outside the boundaries of whiteness for one reason or another, and our experiences were all molded by this fact.

Very few of my teachers were out and out racist, far as I could tell. I was never called a racial slur – by them, to be clear; it's definitely happened – and a lot of the experiences you'll hear about where we were singled out for our behavior or some other reason might not *seem* racial in our retelling, if you haven't had the experience yourself. The reason I am going in depth into these concepts in this introduction is to provide the context necessary to understand that the way our society has been constructed leads to an experience that is unavoidably different from our peers, even if these differences aren't necessarily as dramatic as what you might see on the news.

The impact of racism can often be quite subtle, especially in the classroom. Sometimes it's something you can only feel, and only if you are on the receiving end of it at that. The often-fictional stories our country has written about different racial groups have been told to us through our history books and our movies, and we've all been trained in stereotypes and fears, even me and the other people in this book. Much as you or I might want to tell ourselves we're beyond this training, it's work we have to do every day so we can push back against what we once learned. Formal teacher training includes readings and lessons about all sorts of different scenarios and contexts, but the training that exists doesn't do a good enough job at ensuring all teachers unlearn the stories they've been told about different races. And hey, that's not your fault – my original training on race and education was nonexistent. There are now plenty of wonderful books designed to bridge this gap, but that gap shouldn't exist in the first place, and as long as our racial narratives persist, the unlearning is going to have to continue. On top of all of that, of course, when you add those stories to what people have been told about neurodivergence, what you get is what we experienced as students.

The word *neurodivergent* was coined in 1998 by an Australian sociologist named Judy Singer, proposed as a sort of offshoot to the then-recent concept of *neurodiversity*.[3] You might still come across people who use the now-archaic "neuroatypical" to describe us, but many of us feel that that term defines us by what we aren't or by what we lack, and therefore others us in a way that is detrimental. Some of us don't like the word neurodivergent, but I personally find that it implies a meta-phorical fork in the road and that it therefore provides us with agency we are often denied, and certainly more so than before this and other terms were created. Others prefer terms like *neurospicy*, but I don't love that one because it feels like an ethnic stereotype. More power to those who identify that way, as the point is for us to be able to choose how we want to be seen, an opportunity we rarely receive as neurodivergent people, and neurodivergent people of color in particular. I have also seen people declare that they are *neurodiverse*, but just like *diverse* itself, one person cannot be neurodiverse. Your classroom, however, is probably neurodiverse because there are many different brains and ways of thinking in the group. All of these words, and the others being developed with each passing year, are attempts to get out from under the oppressive language and insults many of us have experienced, so, as far as I'm concerned, they're all better than the alternatives, some of which you'll hear later.

The question of what is included under the extremely large tent of neurodivergence is one that people ask quite often. There is no perfect list, and certainly not one that the American Medical Association (AMA) or American Psychological Association (APA) can accurately provide given that it's not technically a medical term in the first place. But, for the record, the most common forms of neurodivergence include, but are absolutely not limited to: autism spectrum disorder, inclusive of what we used to call Asperger's syndrome until we remembered Asperger was a Nazi; dyslexia, dyscalculia, dysgraphia, and other related challenges; certain types of sensory processing disorders; bipolar disorder and other related conditions (*yes, these are usually considered mental health conditions, but the neurodivergence umbrella is deliberately broad and so I'm including it here*); and of course, attention deficit/hyperactivity disorder. You will notice there is a particular word that recurs in that list, and the prefix "dys-" serves precisely the same purpose, meaning "bad, abnormal, impaired, difficult."[4] You best believe we will get into all of that, but suffice it to say for now that I think it might just be a society that stigmatizes us in this way that is actually bad, even if it is, unfortunately, not abnormal.

A great number of us have more than one, let's just call it for now, condition, with plenty of people I've spoken to identifying themselves as, for example, "AuDHD." We also tend to have higher rates of mental health issues, especially mood disorders like anxiety and depression.[5] My own very, very slow path to an age-35 diagnosis made pit stops in Anxietytown and Depressionburg, not just in how I felt but also in what I thought was "the answer" to my problems. It was clear to anyone who had ever spent time with me that I was pretty visibly anxious, and with growing social acceptance of this issue among younger populations, I felt comfortable sharing that this was true of me. I was probably a little too comfortable, honestly, because I think I sometimes used it as an excuse not to address my struggles. At the same time, for reasons that will become clear throughout the book, I experienced a lot of fairly dark emotional periods, and a pretty constant feeling of social isolation. I did not, for the longest time, consider that I could possibly be depressed. Oh, sure, I *felt* depressed, in an informal sense, but every depiction I saw of depression, both in popular culture and in the few people I knew who admitted to it, they didn't act like me, and they absolutely didn't look like me. The typical – there's that word again – example had trouble getting out of bed, had trouble meeting their obligations, maybe had issues with hygiene, and cried often. In my then-immature way, I figured, if I'm not like that, then I can't be depressed. I usually met my obligations, I was absolutely never late to anything, I was probably a little too concerned with my hygiene because I didn't want to be socially rejected, and I didn't cry between 2004 and early 2016, which I think you might see as a bright red flag as you read this but it was something I was proud of at the time. And so, when, in high school, I would go for long, cold walks around Manhattan wishing I'd been invited to social events, instead of realizing I needed help, I blamed everything on myself. *Of course I didn't get invited*, I would say to myself, *I'm just as annoying as they think I am. I just have to figure out what's wrong with me, and fix it, and I'll be part of the group.*

Knowing what I know now, I think I just got lucky that whatever was going on with me never tipped over into symptoms of major depressive disorder, which a few of the people I interviewed described as having been physically incapacitating; additionally, as a man (or a boy at the time), we do tend to mask our symptoms with outward anger and other acceptably male emotions.[6] But I didn't know any of this back then, so I didn't even consider it possible I needed to tend to my mental health at all.

The thought process I just outlined happens to a lot of us neurodivergent people, and particularly to us NDSOC. And before you ask, I just lied to my parents. I tended to do well enough academically, and I eventually got into a great college, so there never seemed to be much that was visibly "wrong," and my school never thought I needed any support whatsoever. In retrospect, I made it through by the skin of my teeth, white-knuckling my life and trying to stay ahead of how I felt, riding the waves of emotional volatility until after I married my wife and she finally told me to see someone. The second therapist I went to helped me figure out that it was possible I could be depressed, but the neurodivergence conversation still didn't come up for another three years until some of the workplace issues I mentioned in the prologue started happening. Now, I don't even know if it was clinical depression as such – as a Black man who was told he was gifted, it was made clear to me by my institutions that there was never an option to not Get Out of Bed and Get Things Done, so I always did. When I couldn't process something emotionally or motivate myself to finish a dull project, I was told I wasn't trying hard enough, and I believed it. Ultimately, though I'm definitely prone to anxiety, I think, just as is true for a lot of us, I experienced most of my depressive periods because of the messages I received about my supposed inadequacy. But, unfortunately, those periods had cut neural grooves deep enough that the only medication I actually take these days is for my mood and not even for focus and stimulation.

Now, mood disorders are absolutely classified under the label of *disability*, as they are considered medical issues, regardless of their provenance. Since, as mentioned, neurodivergent is not a medical term, does that mean we are disabled? Well, it's important we briefly discuss what that even means. For a great many practitioners, disability denotes a medical issue to be treated and fixed, whereas as for many in the community, what we have is a, let's be clear, real set of issues, but the neurological and physical and emotional challenges are better referred to as *impairments*. While we may still choose to refer to ourselves as disabled – or dis/abled, dis/Abled, *and other related spellings, some of which I use in my academic work* – as a term of solidarity, the only thing that renders us *incapable* in our society is how it has been built to exclude us. For example, you could say that someone who is unable to walk simply has a condition that will make life more challenging, but if our cities and countries were truly accessible, it would not be nearly as much of an impediment. And then, when it comes to neurodivergence, my inability to control my level of focus is definitely a "problem" when I am forced to sit quietly in a fifth-grade classroom, but by the time I eventually ended up in my doctoral program, I got everything done extremely quickly and finished faster than everyone. In other words, impairments are what they are, and for many of us there really are chemical differences in our brains and bodies that set us apart. But these differences only hold us back because the world wasn't built with us in mind, and that absolutely includes our classrooms and our teacher training. What I am trying to say is that we didn't get to this point by accident or by chance, and when you think about the history of this country and the systemic racism involved, the intersection at which we live makes life, and learning, extra challenging. Indeed, the history of America's racism and the history of its ableism isn't really two different stories but a single, ugly, overlapping narrative, which will serve as the final bit of preamble before we get into the body of the book.

A Very Brief History of the Intersection between Ableism and Racism in America

If you are talking about the systemic racism of the United States, you are talking about chattel slavery to some extent, whether you want to be or not. Indeed, you are talking about the broader concept of European colonialism, because both processes were based, in part, on the idea that the people who were captured and enslaved were not mentally capable of governing themselves. Though it presumably seems purely evil in the 2020s to enslave people, there was never a time when everyone involved in the system was willing to accept that they were the moral villains, and part of the way they justified their participation was by categorizing the people they captured as mentally disabled. Accordingly, their slaves were better off being the property of plantation owners, because they couldn't take care of themselves and needed the wisdom of white, wealthy men to keep them on the right path.[7] Additionally, the conquered individuals who managed to demonstrate mimicry of their overlords were classified as more worthwhile.[8] Into this mix was added the reality of slavery and the impact it had on the people who suffered under it.

While enslaved people were considered disabled and therefore deserving of being denied their full humanity, the question of what to do with people who emerged from the institution was rarely front of mind. In the 19th century, though, a few things happened that made it absolutely necessary to answer these questions. Whereas, in the pre- and early colonial periods, people who had various impairments were integrated into society in some fashion[9] – and, amusingly, a lot of us were hired as educators – by the time the 20th century approached, a few things had changed. First, we were in the midst of the industrial revolution, which changed the way we all worked, for better or worse. Additionally, the enormity of the Civil War meant that a significant portion of (male) workers were impacted by the brutal battles the conflict required. It might now be somewhat common to think of veterans as deeply scarred and needing societal support, but the Civil War was the first time in this country's history when this pattern was established systematically. So, between the people who had been freed from a brutal daily existence of bondage and the men who had suffered through the war, there was an astronomical number of individuals who were either physically or mentally impaired that the country had no real idea of how to handle. There were millions of people who were no longer capable of the new sort of productivity that the culture demanded, and as such, what we think of as disability emerged as a way to classify those who couldn't generate value as efficiently as everyone else. The details have shifted since the late 19th century, of course, but I contend that, deep down, our society still views disability, neurodivergence, and neurodivergence among individuals from marginalized groups, as categories that mark its members as less productive and therefore deserving of exclusion.

Around the same time as a new class of impaired individuals was being created, academia was in the process of etching ugly racial "science" into its literature. Before the Civil War, scholar and slaveowner Samuel Cartwright coined the term *drapetomania*, which he defined as the mental illness of seeking freedom from slavery.[10] Even though the term was made irrelevant by the end of American chattel slavery, the underlying idea that seeking liberation was evidence of mental illness persisted among the ranks of the most prestigious of the country's institutions. The eugenics movement, for example, was not *exclusively* racist, but it went a long way towards aligning race and disability as issues to be dealt with by the broader society. We, in the United States, prefer to think of ourselves as more moral than the most genocidal of governments, but the way we clung to and propagated eugenicist ideologies had a tangible impact on other countries in ways that I suspect we'd rather not think about.[11]

Experiments were carried out on Black people, without using the newly developed anesthetics that were starting to be freely distributed. The medical establishment didn't believe we felt pain in the same way as white patients,[12] a strange and discomfiting stereotype that continues to impact doctor–patient relationships to this very day.[13] I am reluctant to traffic in the pain of people of color, but suffice it to say that it has been hundreds of years that we've been seen as disabled by the very fact that we are not white, and so there's little history of race that can be seen as complete if the concept of disability is not part of the discussion. And since we're talking about the late 19th century, do you know what else emerged from that time period? The American public school system! Although I cannot convincingly assert that the racism and ableism of the 19th century is present in our current classrooms, I do think it's instructive to consider the place that our system emerged from if we are to wonder why the NDSOC in this book experienced the things that we did. Indeed, the standards to which we are all held are based on a population that we aren't a part of, and many of our struggles are caused by a monolithic set of expectations that we were almost destined not to meet.

Book Preview

The rest of the book will be arranged in a very specific manner, because as a person with ADHD I can't accomplish something complex and lengthy without forcing myself to be extremely regimented with set, targeted goals. There are 13 chapters after this introduction, and a conclusion. All 13 chapters will have roughly the same structure, and will be about the same length, which would be approximately 4,000 words. I hope that this repetition makes the work easier to process instead of dull, but if you do get bored at some point, understand that the structure was chosen on purpose. Also, for the record, if you are reading this as an emerging scholar, you can think of this as a sort of *collective autoethnography*[14] for pedagogical purposes, or a series of *counter-narratives*.[15]

In this book, each of the chapter titles can be seen as the second half of a sentence that begins, "You might find neurodivergent students of color . . ." I have very little interest in giving the AMA and APA influence over the points I am trying to make, but I thought it would be a useful approach to center on a supposed "symptom" in each chapter and explore the way my interviewees – and I myself – have experienced these tendencies. That, by the way, is the last time you'll see me refer to common traits as such – they are traits we have in common and that's neither bad nor good. In choosing this structure, I hope to debunk what are ultimately race-based assumptions about why, how, and when we, for example, get overwhelmed, or don't complete our homework, or never shut up.

To that end, the chapters are as follows:

◆ **Talking Out of Turn** – Centered on "disruption," this chapter focuses on why we don't always fit into the order of a standardized classroom.
◆ **Making Meaning** – This chapter centers on the unique ways we communicate and/or process language. We are often told we communicate poorly, but the true issue is we are on a wavelength different from most others.

- **Getting Things Done** – This chapter focuses on the way we do or don't manage to complete our assigned tasks and how to support us more effectively in doing so.
- **Coloring Outside the Lines** – On a related note, this chapter is centered on our unique approaches to assigned work and how our unusual ways of completing tasks serve us better than what might be expected of us.
- **Remembering and Forgetting** – This chapter focuses on the variability of memory and how that impacts our educational performance, with the aim to give teachers reading this book more insight into the way we are putting forth our very best effort.
- **Staying Out of View** – This chapter focuses on the way that socialization impacts different subgroups, in particular women and others who are assigned female at birth. Whereas someone like me would always tell a joke in class to avoid doing homework, my female NDSOC classmates might have tried to stay fully in the shadows.
- **Following Recipes** – One of the most difficult things for me and many others like me to do is follow long, complex instructions, which is a skill that is certainly required in education.
- **Turning the Volume Down** – This chapter is about sensory overload, and how that can obviously be an obstacle but can also push us forward when we are supported effectively.
- **Trying to Catch the Express Train** – This chapter is about the often wild swings between chaos and hyperfocus that we experience and how teachers can help us tap into the latter.
- **Catching Our Breath** – This chapter is focused on our emotional volatility, something I've already mentioned in this introduction. I do not think we are naturally prone to these issues, but the system built around us pushes us into corners that cause us to react in unpredictable ways, and this chapter explores that pattern.

- **Being an Easy Target** – The perception of social rejection has had far too much of an influence on my life, and for many of us, this is a deeply impactful experience that most outside of the neurodivergent community might not understand. My hope with this chapter is to shed light on why we feel this way.
- **Beating Ourselves Up** – This chapter centers on guidance for readers in identifying how we might be expressing our shame, and how teachers can build us up when we've already torn ourselves down.
- **Outrunning the Pack** – And finally, the body of the book will end with an unequivocally positive chapter which will center on the ways that, when we are placed into supportive situations, we can outperform anyone and everyone.
- Following this, as mentioned, there will be a conclusion summarizing the ideas contained in the previous 13 chapters. So, as teachers, this conclusion is positioned as an example of how you can be the educator that NDSOC see as a path forward, a bridge to reaching the potential that our institutions have often prevented us from seeing.

Hopefully, this structure will allow this book to be both readable and compelling, but ultimately what matters is that it helps the students who are similar to the kid I once was. I want nothing more than for these students to feel like they are loved and protected in their classrooms instead of isolated and ignored, or, worse, singled out and shamed. By reading this, you are doing right by these students, and by the end of the book, you should have ideas about how you can support us more effectively. Let's get going then.

Notes

1 Painter, N. (2011) *The History of White People*. New York: W.W. Norton.
2 Loewen, J. (2005) *Sundown Towns: A Hidden Dimension of American Racism*. New York: The New Press.

3   https://my.clevelandclinic.org/health/symptoms/23154-neurodivergent
4   https://www.collinsdictionary.com/us/dictionary/english/dys
5   https://www.psychologytoday.com/us/blog/pathways-progress/202108/is-there-link-between-neurodiversity-and-mental-health
6   Martin, L.A., Neighbors, H.W., and Griffith, D.M. (2013) The Experience of Symptoms of Depression in Men vs Women: Analysis of the National Comorbidity Survey Replication. *JAMA Psychiatry* 70 (10), 1100–1106. doi:10.1001/jamapsychiatry.2013.1985
7   Nielsen, K. (2012) *A Disability History of the United States*. Boston, MA: Beacon Press.
8   Mills, C. and Lefrancois, B. (2018) Child as Metaphor: Colonialism, Psygovernance, and Epistemicide. *World Futures* 74 (7–8), 503–524.
9   Nielsen, K. (2012) *A Disability History of the United States*. Boston, MA: Beacon Press.
10 Willoughby, C. (2018) Running Away from Drapetomania: Samuel A. Cartwright, Medicine, and Race in the Antebellum South. *Journal of Southern History* 84 (3), 579–614.
11 United States Holocaust Memorial Museum (n.d.) Holocaust Encyclopedia. The Biological State: Nazi Racial Hygiene: 1933–1939. See https://encyclopedia.ushmm.org/content/en/article/the-biological-state-nazi-racial-hygiene-1933-1939.
12 Sayej, N. (2018, April 21) J Marion Sims: Controversial Statue Taken Down But Debate Still Rages. *The Guardian*. See https://www.theguardian.com/artanddesign/2018/apr/21/j-marion-sims-statue-removed-new-york-city-black-women.
13 https://www.nytimes.com/2019/11/25/upshot/opioid-epidemic-blacks.html.
14 https://www.apa.org/pubs/books/essentials-autoethnography-sample-chapter.pdf
15 See https://www.ndbooks.com/book/counternarratives/ for more examples

1

Talking Out of Turn

On Being Seen as a Classroom Disruption

For most of my childhood and a good portion of my adolescence, the school I attended was a "quirky" place that didn't have letter grades at all. Yes, sure, if I took a test in math class they would tell me how many I got wrong or right, and I usually did well on those sorts of assignments if I bothered to put in any effort. The first time I got a letter grade – *an A-, as it turns out* – was my freshman year of college, when I took a French class that was too easy for me and set myself up for some trouble when I interpreted this performance to mean that all of college wouldn't require focus or hard work. Oops.

Anyway, when I was a younger child, though, and home-work truly wasn't rigorous, the only evaluation I really received was qualitative narratives about what sort of presence I was in the classroom. I'm sure they assessed my performance too, but the only thing that seemed consistent enough from semester to semester was that I "talked out of turn." Perhaps because everyone at the school was supposed to be intellectually advanced, this was the only thing that stood out enough about me to (literally) write home about – the fact that I talked too much and at the wrong times.

DOI: 10.4324/9781003465126-2

I'm not going to do this every single chapter, but if you go to the DSM-5 (Diagnostic and Statistical Manual of Mental Disorders, Volume 5) summary of ADHD,[1] among our common traits you will find the following:

- ◆ Often talks excessively.
- ◆ Often blurts out an answer before a question has been completed.
- ◆ Often has trouble waiting their turn.
- ◆ Often interrupts or intrudes on others (e.g., butts into conversations or games).

I'm not going to sit here and pretend this wasn't true of me, but I ask you, as you read this, what does it mean to talk "excessively"? I wonder if we're expecting each child to speak for 1/15th (or 1/20th, or 1/30th) of the time the teacher isn't speaking. And I wonder if teachers can calculate precisely when a student has or hasn't stepped over their allotted speech limit; after all, studies have shown educators pay closer attention to non-white students' supposed misbehavior starting as early as pre-school.[2] While you're considering this, I will share with you one of the ways this reputation for excessive noise translated into gaining an academic reputation as a nuisance.

Counter-Narratives

By sixth grade, I had become a student who was more concerned with being socially accepted than completing homework assignments. Because I was utterly hopeless at understanding most social dynamics, I mostly tried to make people laugh, partially to hide when I was confused or had misunderstood the material. My sixth grade history teacher, Mr. O'Donnell (all names, unless otherwise indicated, are pseudonyms), was a tough but well-respected educator who had a practice of assigning us vocabulary to look up in the dictionary based on things that happened in the classroom, and this was actual work because this was long before you could instantly do this on a smartphone; you really had to crack open a physical book. One day, being as clumsy as a lot of folks with ADHD are, I dropped my pencil, and, to hide my embarrassment, I tried to make a joke out of it by chasing after it on the floor. No one laughed, and, glaring at me, Mr. O'Donnell stated flatly, "To irk," meaning he wanted us to come to the next class having memorized what it meant. Because I rarely did my homework back then, it took me until that next class to realize he was helping my classmates remember a synonym for "annoying" by associating it with me. On the one hand, I still bristle when called "annoying" or anything similar, but on the other hand, I guess if his goal was to ensure we remembered the vocabulary, he succeeded, because I'll never forget what "irk" means. So, good job, I guess, Mr. O'Donnell.

"I think I always had 'talked too much' on my report card," Marie told me when I asked her about this. Marie is a doctoral student of Indigenous descent who was raised in Oklahoma, and she was in her late 20s at the time of our conversation. Her school was mostly white, with a few fellow Indigenous students, and "I don't think there was a single Black student in my grade growing up.

"I was not diagnosed until I was an adult," Marie said, echoing a common theme for everyone included here. "But looking back it's pretty evident that I have had ADHD all my life. And I'm actually in the process now of doing a full neuropsych evaluation to better understand whether or not I [also] have autism . . . It's a fairly new diagnosis, but it has brought a lot of, I think, insight into the way my mind works and into the way it has always worked and different barriers that I faced in the past make a lot more sense now that I know I have ADHD." If you recall the prologue, that's that sense of relief I felt with my own relatively new diagnosis.

"I wasn't necessarily the disruptive kid in the sense that I was like fidgeting too much, or, like distracting my peers other than trying to talk too much. I was, quote, unquote, a good student. Like, I had great grades," she explained. "In my head, I guess thinking if we're gonna learn about a subject let's discuss it and indulge with that subject and go for it. But I guess it came at the expense of the teachers being able to teach or at the expense of the students being able to listen is the way it was viewed."

I want to pause here and consider her final statement there. Clearly, being talkative is not inherently bad (or good). What mattered, for Marie and for all of us, was "the way it was viewed." As far as I'm concerned, unless we're told explicitly at the start of a school year or semester that there is a specific amount we're supposed to speak according to a defined rubric – which seems unlikely – then the only reason to criticize us for doing so is because it's subjectively irritating or causes some objective and codified issue. There is obviously a limit that you'll need to decide for yourselves when managing a classroom, but unless we can state for certain that how much we speak is hindering others' comprehension, all we're doing by reminding neurodivergent students of color that we talk too much is making us feel worse than we often already do.

"My teachers liked me," Marie added. "Because I had good grades. So they thought, okay, she's a good kid . . . So it was, it was a caveat of like she's doing well, but in the sense that yes, she's talking too much."

Like everyone I spoke to, Marie was not diagnosed until after her adolescence – in her case, she was 26 – and so there was no official policy for her teachers or school to follow in supporting her. And so, especially as long as she performed well, the only thing that really stuck out was how much she spoke.

Thinking back to how others were viewed for similar behavior, Marie told me about other talkative students she'd gone to school with. "There were a couple that were like me that were the gifted kids that talked too much, but they weren't always chastised in the same manner," she recounted. "And I think a lot of that also had to do with the fact that a lot of times they were boys. So I know that that plays into a lot of this and I think being a girl I was expected to behave a certain way and when I did it, that was disciplined a little bit more."

Like Marie, I had classmates who talked just as much or more than I did and were nonetheless given support instead of being made an example of. I certainly can't say it was my gender that led to my being singled out, but my classmates absolutely fit the neurodivergent stereotype of white boys who were unable to sit still. I even had a classmate who was prone to folding himself into a pretzel shape when frustrated. Part of my goal here is not to say these other students should have been punished for the way they were comfortable existing, but to point out that we notice when we're treated differently, even if it doesn't come off as deliberately cruel in the moment.

Ellie is a Cuban-American neuroscientist from Massachusetts in her early 30s who considers herself white-presenting (that is, fair-skinned). I by no means attempted to cast a particularly wide net for this book, as this is a small set of interviews rather than a more comprehensive comparative study, but I should note here that, although, aside from possibly Ellie herself, none of us would ever be *mistaken* for white, none of us are relatively dark-skinned, myself included. As I mentioned in the introduction, the trajectories of the people I interviewed are objectively impressive, as is the work they've done thus far in their careers. And a small, sad part of me expects that part of our success has been due to the way that colorism might have slightly blunted the impacts of racism on our lives.

"I was kind of thinking about . . . what my academic identity was," Ellie told me, "and I think it was also super salient to me that I was Cuban-American and that I was like, different. [Hometown] was so homogenous for the most part and I was thinking about how I think because of the cultural difference, I was a little bit also empowered to be different, or be unique, because I already recognized that.

"I do think I had both a sense of pride but also sometimes jealousy for some of the things my friends who were white had," she said. "But I think that I basically . . . I was loud. I was excitable, I was like, I could probably have a little bit of that hand up, you know, the 'me! me!' hand and all of that."

Speaking again of her politically progressive hometown, she said, "There were a lot of multicultural celebrations, a lot of reading books, and 'this person's Mom's going to bring in this food from this culture' or something like that. So I do think I was lucky that compared to a lot of other places I could have been at least it was like celebrated to be different."

Ellie has thought about her experience deeply, especially since attaining her advanced degrees, and she's able to analyze her behavior with some academic expertise. "There's actually this construct called behavioral activation," she explained to me, which was the first time I'd heard of it. "It's an approach towards reward and an increase that can be associated with bipolar [disorder]," which she's been diagnosed with. Behavioral activation can also apparently be used to support the treatment of depression.[3] Later chapters will explore how we do or don't motivate ourselves to complete assigned tasks, so this won't be the last I write about systems of rewards.

"I was so into school," she continued. "Participating in everything and I'm sure that it was because of the social rewards like with teachers, that was the key reason that I think I cared more, not necessarily even as much as like learning outcomes." It's certainly not a bad thing for your teachers to like you, but it's certainly not the sole intent of schooling. Accordingly, while she wasn't seen as "disruptive" in the way that Marie and I were, this focus on approval did have an impact on her.

"I would be really anxious if I would get in trouble for anything," she said. "One time I stole a cookie as a kindergartener. Then they said they were gonna tell my parents and I felt sick for days waiting."

You may be catching an undercurrent of the emotional toll this took on us, and while there is far more about this in later chapters, I hope readers can start to note that, whether we're talking "too much," not enough, or even just the right amount, it's rarely driven by a brazen disregard for others or a lack of social graces.

Terry is a law librarian in their – Terry uses they/them pronouns – late 40s who was raised in Trinidad. They, like most of the rest of us in this book, were far ahead of their peers academically as a young child and did well on most official assessments.

"Our teachers were not necessarily qualified to teach," Terry explained. "And so I had teachers who had very varying levels of experience in teaching and abilities. So I had one teacher who the way she taught is she walked into the room and wrote onto the board the information that we needed to know that week. And when she got to the bottom of the board, she erased the top and started writing again. And that was how she taught us biology.

"I had a physics teacher who required us to memorize verbatim the words in the textbook and to rewrite it exactly as in the textbook on the test. And if you change 'the' for an 'a' or paraphrasing, in your own words, you were deducted marks for every word that was different from what was in the book . . . So I taught myself a lot of things from the textbooks. And because I couldn't remember when assignments were due or when tests were going to come up in class, I sort of coasted on my innate intelligence during the school year.

"I was at the top of my class and every single subject that I was taking, because I had been teaching myself out of the textbook and also I had tutors that my dad hired to give me extra lessons outside of the class. So I didn't necessarily have to be able to pay attention in class to be able to do well on my exams."

And so, you might think that a student skilled enough to need very little academic coaching would hardly have been seen as a disruption, and they weren't seen as loud in the same way that Marie or I was. But nevertheless, their teachers found a way to be irritated by Terry's presence.

"I would say," Terry told me, "I was mostly not disruptive in the classroom other than the fact that I am sensitive to light. And so I needed to wear sunglasses, which some of my teachers felt my sunglasses were disruptive because it was like the late 80s. And they were fluorescent yellow, and so they made me switch to a more neutral pair of sunglasses so that I would be less disruptive."

One of the things I've learned about myself since my diagnosis is that the years I spent not quite being able to figure out how to blend in – because it's not actually possible for folks like us, I know now – have made me a bit wary of people potentially scrutinizing me. These days, I always want to feel in control of how much attention I am and am not attracting, and one of the ways I do that is by favoring very bright colors, which, yes, includes a fair amount of yellow. In a way it feels sort of defiant not to try and hide. I mention this because Terry clearly just wanted to get through their school day without being disturbed (by light in this case), and the way they were comfortable sitting in the classroom, despite not making any supposedly excessive noise, was still too much for some of their teachers to handle. I say again, it's not as though none of us are ever genuinely disruptive – Terry even told me about a fight they got into after another student insulted them – so much as a common refrain that even when we're just trying to learn, the way we are doesn't match the way we're supposed to be.

It wasn't always bad, though. Sometimes we encountered teachers who were able to handle the fact that we were, as the kids say, Extra. Marie told me of one of the ways a teacher of hers channeled her curiosity into a positive moment in class.

"I remember when we learned about what a mole was in chemistry," she said. "And it's like this measurement for however much. I don't even remember . . ." (*It's a standard unit for measuring "large quantities of very small entities." Yes, I had to look that up – I wasn't paying much attention in chemistry class.*[4]) "So, you know, we calculated how many moles of something it would take to cover the tennis court outside of our classroom and I was like, 'Well, how many would it take to get to the sun?' And so she said, 'Yeah, let's do that math.' So she Googled how many miles it was from Earth to the Sun. And then we went and did that entire calculation together as a class.

"So instead of saying, 'we don't have time for your questions, [Marie],' she actually took that question as a learning opportunity for the rest of the class instead of just saying, you know, 'well, we've got to move on and we don't have time for this pointless calculation of how many moles of whatever it would take to reach the sun.' Like it was exciting because she made it exciting."

Marie is a few years younger than I am, just enough of an age difference that my teachers couldn't have easily Googled anything in the classroom. Accordingly, it was harder for them to find a way to soak up the extra mental energy I had trouble controlling. By the time I got to high school, though, my goofing off had tapered enough that I had started trying to be an actor, and while I can't say I was all that . . . good at it, I threw myself into it with gusto, like I do with everything I'm temporarily obsessed with. Since it was such a small school, my teachers knew this about me – some of them watched the school plays – and my English teachers started calling on me to make up voices for characters in the novels we read, which was one of the first times I remember eliciting genuine laughter from my classmates, or at least laughter that wasn't at my expense.

Whatever our particular curiosities are, they're unlikely to be contained within the boundaries of the curriculum, and teachers have a choice to either indulge our intellectual rabbit holes or try to curtail them. As Terry told me, "I think that some of my teachers themselves were bullies. I had an art teacher that would walk by my desk and tell me things like, 'what are you making, a mess?'" I doubt anyone reading this book would talk to a student that way, but if you consider that somewhere along the line, an educator has probably considered us disruptive, then it might fall to you to support a person who's had this experience in their past. Indeed, they might be having it in one of their other classes right now. You'll have to make the choice yourself as to whether Googling how many tennis balls it would take to reach the sun – *no, I am not doing that math* – is a valuable use of time or not, and I'm certain it will depend on the specific circumstances when such a question comes up in class, but Marie remembers how she felt when her ideas weren't dismissed, and I do too.

Ellie mentioned that, while her hometown was nominally liberal and therefore accepting of different demographics to some extent, sometimes her neurodivergent tendencies were ascribed to her "culture." "I think," she said, "if I had any further challenges like that it totally laughed it off and was . . . attributed to just like, I'm just like *different*. I'm just like, more relaxed than other people because I'm Cuban or something like that." Of course, that's the sort of thing that happens when there aren't very many of a group in a classroom – we often have to stand in for everyone who looks like us, and so, while we might be behaving a certain way, or talking a certain amount, because of the parts of our brains we don't have the tools to understand, it can get chalked up to another way that we differ from the unmentioned standard. In other words, because we don't resemble the neurodivergent norm, the ways we stand out are rarely ascribed to a neurodivergence we haven't been diagnosed with. I, for one, was not only Black, but also small in stature and a year younger than my classmates – *of course*, the school figured, *he might struggle to connect with his peers.* Not that they really did anything to help, but neurodivergence wasn't even considered a possibility so long as we could memorize enough information to keep progressing through school.

It's certainly important to understand and be respectful of all students' cultures, but when it crosses over into stereo-typing, it can pigeonhole us into roles that don't actually suit us effectively. Are there cultures where overlapping dialogue is more common than others? Sure. But then when everything we do in the classroom is seen through the lens of our racial and cultural identity, we still aren't given the opportunity to be the full individuals we are. I know I'm advocating for readers to pay attention to the intersection of racism and ableism, so you might be thinking, how can I avoid being color-evasive while also not seeing everything as downstream of our cultures? And it's hard! The best way I can describe this is as a balan-cing act between respecting our cultures and racial identities while keeping in mind that what could be criticized as talking out of turn might be a byproduct of neurodivergence or some-thing similar. Or both. Frankly, you may never know why we do what we do, and, especially as younger children, we prob-ably don't know either, but, unless we truly cross some sort of line in the classroom, we need to be given the space to indulge in our many, many curiosities. As much extra work as it might seem like it would take to give us a few extra minutes here or there, it would take just as much time trying to keep us quiet, and it wouldn't even work.

Takeaways

Also on the DSM's list of common ADHD traits is the statement "often 'on the go' acting as if 'driven by a motor.'" And I can tell you as I near 40 years of age, there's no real way to turn that motor off. We can try and suppress it, but then it'll spin in circles inside of our heads and we won't be able to accomplish anything at all, certainly nothing we're not already deeply interested in. The best thing teachers can do for us is to help us point our own motors in the right direction. Or, in the metaphor I've started using for myself and that you'll hear throughout the book, give us the train tracks our brains need to reach full speed.

"I started writing stories and they were a little bit beyond what the teacher would ask for," Marie said. "And she started encouraging it, rather than telling me like, 'that's not what the prompt was.' It was very much like, Okay, well, you went off, and it actually worked really well. And it was a really good little story. I wrote one about my sister's dog and my uncle's dog and how they had like little adventures and I still have like the original manuscript of it, like five or six pages printed out. It's got an oil stain on it, but I cherish it because it was one of those first moments where I wrote something for fun *for me*. And I think I was encouraged to continue writing but that kind of got overshadowed in high school by you know, just everything that was demanded of me from other classes."

I understand that, especially without an IEP (those will be mentioned eventually if you are looking for that), it might take considerable trial and error to help a student like those you've met in this chapter find out what "train tracks" might help their motor run as smoothly as possible, and who has time for that? If there are four to five Maries or Ellies in your classroom and they're getting good enough grades while other students are struggling, why bother to put oil on the wheels that aren't squeaking? You're not going to verbally abuse a student the way Terry was abused, so why not just focus on your presumably astronomical amount of responsibilities? Choosing either of the extremes mentioned here – telling us to be quiet or chalking up our garrulousness to What We Do In Our Culture – is easier than the messy and imprecise work of supporting us.

If you have students of color who you might otherwise simply evaluate as talking out of turn, instead take the time to encourage us to explore non-curricular interests in the classroom. The amount of time "wasted" by following us into tangents will be made up for by the speed with which we will likely grasp concepts in the long run so long as we are mentally stimulated, and these detours will hopefully help with that.

Write down our "train tracks" and try to place us on them when we seem like we're veering into a mental ditch. And don't be surprised if you have to keep updating your lists of train tracks, because what helps our motors run smoothly in September might not work in October, and I know that's frustrating to hear and to have to do, but believe you me, it's even more frustrating to experience.

If we really want to talk about something we're excited by, no matter how off-topic it seems, make a deal with us and give us a certain amount of time to brain dump. Maybe you give us a few minutes in each class, or once a week, what have you, with few if any restrictions other than a timeframe. *You* may or may not find it annoying, but I assure you *we* will find it very meaningful.

Notes

1   https://www.cdc.gov/ncbddd/adhd/diagnosis.html
2   Sabol, T.J., Kessler, C.L., Rogers, L.O., Petitclerc, A., Silver, J., Briggs-Gowan, M., et al. (2022) A Window into Racial and Socioeconomic Status Disparities in Preschool Disciplinary Action Using Developmental Methodology. *Annals of the New York Academy of Sciences* 1508, 123–136.
3   https://www.psychologytools.com/self-help/behavioral-activation/
4   https://www.britannica.com/science/mole-chemistry

2

Making Meaning
On the Unique Ways We Communicate

Although *neurodivergent* is not a medical term, there is still, rightfully, guidance from different corners of the medical community on how to engage with and support us. The Cleveland Clinic, for example, has a somewhat helpful and accessible mini-article defining the term.[1] Under the sub-heading "What are some things I can do to support people who are neurodivergent?" there is a list of six fairly broad takeaways. The second item on the list focuses on communication, and reads: "Communicate in ways that help them. Sometimes, people who are neurodivergent prefer written communication such as instant messaging, texting or emails over a phone call or face-to-face conversation. Give them the time and tools they need to communicate." That's all well and good, but later on in the list there is the following bit of advice: "No two neurodivergent people are the same. The personalities and preferences of neurodivergent people can be widely different, even when they have the same underlying condition." The fact that no two neurodivergent people (of color) are the same is the reason why I based this book around in-depth interviews rather than statistics, but also, even with regards to communication specifically, what we prefer and what we can't stand is wildly

DOI: 10.4324/9781003465126-3

different. This chapter centers on how we try to understand and be understood, how that showed up for us in school, and how the ways we make meaning differ but share common threads.

Counter-Narratives

Seventh grade is when school finally sent me the message that not doing homework and memorizing *just* enough to do well on major exams wasn't going to cut it anymore. That was the year when we had to learn how to do something called a "research paper" and also when one of the primary learning outcomes was our ability to take a large quantity of notes. I use the word "quantity" on purpose, because they sure didn't take the time to teach us how to take *good* notes. Frankly, though, I'm not sure anyone can be prescriptive in how best to take notes – the only person who really knows that is you. The best notes, at least as far as your own learning is concerned, are whatever version helps you understand and/or retain the information and lessons. But that's not what Mr. Rossi cared about.

I remind you that this was before we all had laptops to use in class. Mr. Rossi was teaching us what I guess was a giant cross-section of European history, wars and feudalism and the type of things that certain factions of society insist are more important than stories with people of color in them. We had a textbook that made my back hurt when I carried it home, and we spent most of each class copying down exactly what he wrote on the board, similar to how Terry described the way her biology teacher taught in the previous chapter. Not only did I have illegible handwriting – it's even worse now that I type everything – but it was extremely hard to follow what he was doing because if I got distracted for even one moment, he'd moved onto the next paragraph and I could never catch up to where he was. Far as I could tell, all the other students dutifully followed along (though I bet there were a few other kids who were confused), and he wasn't exactly the type of teacher you could ask for help or lenience. Just like Mr. O'Donnell, he was one of the most respected educators in the school, someone people raved about. Every single day I saw his name on my schedule, I grew deeply anxious and tried not to think about it. I did the best I could to keep pace, but I always missed something important, and he'd grow angry at me when I did poorly on the tests, most of which were essentially checking how well we'd taken notes. This is one of the few times my lack of letter grades saved me, because I'm pretty sure I would have failed. I didn't talk out of turn in that class, though; I just didn't talk at all unless he forced me to admit aloud that I hadn't been following along.

Looking back, there were a lot of reasons why I couldn't do what was asked of me, none of which were a lack of effort. First of all, it wasn't exactly riveting, and I know now that if I'm not into something I'm going to lose interest real fast. Additionally, I cannot copy down more than highlights of what people say or write, at least not at a fast speed, and certainly not in seventh grade when I didn't have a computer in front of me. These days, in work meetings if I have to take notes – and, since I'm open about my diagnosis at my current job, they rarely ask me to – the best I can manage is bullet points, and it seems to go fine for my busy colleagues. At my last job, one of the things that preceded my decision to seek an ADHD evaluation was my supervisor's frustration and fury with how bad my notes were, and I couldn't exactly explain this without seeming just as lazy as she thought I was.

Rachel is a Mexican-American academic in her mid-30s who, say it again with me now, wasn't diagnosed until she was a decade into adulthood. She shared a couple things with me about the way she tends to communicate, one more social and another more related to classroom needs. Regarding the former, she said, "I repeat myself. I also do the thing where to connect with someone I will tell them something very personal about myself when they say something about themselves that I can connect with. So it's not that I want to take the attention away from them. It's just that's the way I can connect with people and let them know that I'm actually paying attention." This sort of, to briefly use more pathologizing language, impulsive oversharing is hardly uncommon, and the flipside is that it can be harder for us to connect and stay engaged when we're prevented from doing this. "It's definitely a matter of deeper connection and it's hard for me to kind of be in the other person's shoes if they're not neurodivergent and don't have this divergent way of thinking because I really do think it's such a good way to connect with people, to share something about yourself in that way. So I definitely struggle with that because I don't understand how other people don't see it the same way." The social isolation that can result from this communication style will be covered later, but consider that, even if it's a classroom lesson rather than a conversation with a peer, something structured as a one-way, passive learning experience is going to be a particular challenge for the way our brains work.

Similar to what I wrote about Mr. Rossi's class, Rachel shared that she felt confused but unable to seek support. "I was already afraid to ask questions," she explained, "because I didn't want to admit that I didn't know anything, that I didn't know something or couldn't figure it out. I also have a hard time formulating questions in my head during classes, because things would go so quickly and I was trying to keep things in my head and they would disappear."

Now, for Rachel, verbal instruction was very hard to follow, and at the end of the chapter we'll return to her and her advice to teachers. As the introductory paragraphs explained though, not all of us are challenged by verbal instruction, and in fact some of us prefer it.

Ellie, the neuroscientist, told me, "I do think that I was quite a slow reader and I have wondered as an adult if there was something a little bit more there but I would therefore have to bullshit all the time that I read stuff that I hadn't read. And I definitely thought I was just a lazy reader. Which I don't really think about it that way as an adult now.

"And verbal explanations are much better for me," she continued. "I did like to write as a kid but reading, not so much." No two neurodivergent people of color are the same, indeed.

To further complicate our wide array of possible needs and strategies, Terry described the extremely labor-intensive process they had to use to process verbal communication, as well as their need for directness, which many of us expressed. I tried to find a way to break up this quote, but honestly, I think you should just read it for yourself.

> Giving directions – like directions to do something or directions on where to go – I need that written down because by the time you've gotten to the end of your directions, I've forgotten the beginning. And it doesn't help for me to pay attention "more" or listen "harder" or try "harder." To the point where the way that I got through school and having to sit in lectures, was, I would also write everything that the teacher was saying – my handwriting was terrible, but I would just write every-thing that they were saying. And when I got home that night, I would transcribe everything using my computer; I would type up what happened in the class. And that's when I would figure out what the topic was. Also, some-times when there were dense topics, I couldn't do the reading ahead of class. So like for my psychology class, I couldn't do the reading ahead of class because I didn't understand what I was reading. And then in terms of communication, I tend to be very direct and practical. And I focused on the words, so people will often read between the lines, things that aren't there and project their meaning onto me so they will project onto me what they would mean if they were saying that in this particular context, when what I mean is the literal words coming out of my mouth. So that creates a lot of problems, espe-cially when over time you're in relationship with the same people and they decide that you mean something. They decide that you're hostile because you're being clear and direct. And so after they make that decision, everything that you say after that gets viewed through the lens of the angry Black person, or in my case, because I'm femme-presenting, as the angry Black woman, which makes it almost impossible to do any kind of repair to the relationship once they've made up their mind who they think I am. I believe that if I were a white man saying the exact same words, they would understand that I am just

being clear and direct and see me as assertive rather than
as angry and hostile.

What you're seeing here is the connection between what is ultimately an issue with the ways our brains work and force us to
process information, which is most likely a biological difference
from the supposed standard, and the impact that our intersectional identities can have on the way this support need is
perceived. Rachel already said that she didn't feel comfortable
asking questions, as was true of me, and Terry had to invent an
entire complex system to get their work done. And yet somehow
they think we're not trying hard enough.

I should point out here that some of the guidance in this
book thus far surely sounds like examples of Universal Design,
and yes, said principles would absolutely benefit us. To me,
the difference is that because of how we present, we're often
assumed not to need support, and when we do struggle, we're
ignored or dismissed as disruptive, or blamed for not trying
hard enough to understand. The ways our racial identities con-
tort our experiences have to remain present and explicit when
considering how best to care for us, and that is an important part
of my goal in sharing these narratives and takeaways with whoever may be reading this.

Whitney is a non-profit manager from Michigan in her early
30s. She told me that her school was relatively diverse, a contrast with some of the others we've met thus far, yet this wasn't
enough to prevent the challenges that most of us had. Regarding
communication, she said, "A lot of times I am repeating things
back to people, kind of confirming what I heard is what I heard,
or asking for someone to repeat something just because I am
picking up on things sometimes a little bit slower or like processing them faster." This last part here is important to note,
as it's not always about us falling behind the class, but is often
that our minds have run off to some future place that's similarly
disconnected from the lesson at hand.

"I'm trying to make sure I understand what is being said,"
Whitney continued. "Or oftentimes, I think, I am speaking too
fast. So I might say something back again, just to make sure folks

are understanding what I'm communicating, and summarizing things a lot at the end because I tend to ramble or I feel like I'm rambling. So then at the end, I'll be like, 'so just to summarize what I said,' and say it again." Considering how often I worry I'm misunderstood and repeat myself accordingly, I assure you that a lot of people do find this, shall we say, irksome, but it's really not our fault, hard as we may try to communicate in a way that works for everyone else.

Ellie shared something similar. "I think what type of feedback I would get a lot is that my stories would be too long, too winding like you'd have too many pitstops along them and I would get that from friends and I remember those comments would be really biting because it was like, 'oh shit, are my stories not interesting?'"

There is a tension you might have noticed, especially if you read Terry's story carefully. Many of us greatly prefer clear and direct communication, but we are also known for rambling, and so it may seem confusing from an outside perspective why the people who might be giving you every piece of information under the sun would like to be communicated with in this way. The best explanation I can give you is that what the world sees as relevant and what our brains see as relevant are very different, and when we seem like we're babbling and repeating ourselves, we really just want to make sure you don't misunderstand us, even though it's probably going to happen anyway.

Marie explained it this way: "I was always told that I talked way too fast. So what was common is I was talking too fast or I was like overloading people with information. So I would have an idea, get really excited about it, and then I would just info dump and the reality is my peers around me couldn't process the info that I was dumping the same way that I could process that info. And I was always talking too fast or too, too, too much or too densely I guess."

To bring this all the way back to Mr. Rossi and similar contexts, the problem was that that was not a compelling activity. I'm not saying there is nothing that could be interesting about European history, but it was one, repetitive act, for most of an entire school year. When we're in educational contexts like this, even those much less extreme in their monotony, then yes, please just tell us what is absolutely necessary without forcing us to read in between the lines. And the end result isn't always just losing interest or boredom, which is probably somewhat inevitable during a given school day. Indeed, our tendency for finding ourselves amidst miscommunication can have a lasting impact.

Marie told me about a lesson she took to heart about communication. "I usually took AP classes," she said, "and that semester, I couldn't because I had a scheduling conflict. And so I, you know, I was used to being the one that like, jumped forward with the answer and then when the rest of my peers did it, I felt bad because the teacher started yelling at us. And I was like, 'Okay, well, I know the answer. I'm just gonna raise my hand and try to get us all out of this yelling situation.'

"And I raised my hand and the teacher said, '[Marie], are you ever gonna let anybody else answer for a change?' And I felt bad because I thought I was trying to help with the situation and like, yeah, I knew the answer. But it wasn't just that it was that the teacher was yelling at us and I was seeing it as an escape option, you know, and that was a case where I learned early on even if you know the answer, and you're being called on appropriately, sometimes you have to dial it back because the teacher is intimidated by how much info you're spouting or how often you know the answer."

I can see how the occasionally harsh statements the interviewees share about their teachers and classroom experiences may put some readers off. If it helps, you might translate her use of "intimidated" into "overwhelmed," but I wanted to leave the actual quote there because that's exactly how it feels from our perspective. Is our perspective the objective truth? Not necessarily, but then neither is the way we are perceived by our institutions, and, though it took me a while, I came to trust our own way of seeing ourselves over what we'd been told was wrong with us, all of which is why these sections are called "counter-narratives."

"If I'm being asked a question," Marie explained, "I'm assuming you want an answer, but I've learned like, especially as an adult I've learned that that is not the script that neurotypicals always follow. A lot of the questions can be rhetorical, and it's better to know when they're rhetorical and when they're not.

"An instance that happened as an adult, it was like, 'why didn't you do XYZ?' and I didn't realize they were asking that to shame me. I'm thinking they're asking because they actually want to know why I didn't do XYZ. So in that instance, I was apparently volunteering too much information because it's more information than the person wanted. But I'm just answering the question you asked. I don't understand why that is a bad thing."

Neither do I.

Takeaways

The people I interviewed certainly had a lot to say about how to address miscommunication. And, as I said above, not all of their suggestions quite coalesce, and that's fine, because ultimately, whatever you decide to do to support the neurodivergent students of color in your classroom is going to depend on the particular ones in front of you. Are they more like Terry? Or Ellie? Or Whitney? Or Marie? Or me?

The issue of potential miscommunication doesn't always become an issue *during* the class in question, too. For a lot of us, we can kind of skate by for a while, either by creating systems the way Terry did, or by asking a friend for help, which shouldn't really be our peers' responsibility. It's sort of a ticking time bomb, though. Even if we make it through middle school and high school, at some point we're going to be thrown into the deep end and forced to figure it all out for ourselves. As Whitney told me about her undergraduate years, "I was trying to find ways to cope with how much information was being kind of thrown at me and how much I was not prepared for college in a lot of ways, even though I was a really good student."

One of the simplest suggestions offered, by a few of the people I spoke to, was to *use multiple modalities* whenever possible. Now, I say "simple" because it's straightforward, not because it doesn't take additional labor. It's easy to remember to flick the subtitles on if you show a documentary in class or share one for homework – and you should absolutely do that – but you aren't going to be able to have a pristine transcript of every extemporaneous thing you say in the classroom. But, as Rachel explained, "I always appreciated when there was subtitles and you know, that's that. That just seems like an easy accommodation for a lot of people, or for a lot of students at a certain age obviously, because I was able to read the subtitles and pay attention to the images and I know that some people can't." None of these takeaways are meant to be perfect fits for every student or class, but that's just one way to support us. It may seem obvious in the sense that for hearing-impaired students this would be done without question, but since we are unlikely to ask for this help or have the accommodation written down for us, just assume someone wants this and turn them on. As Whitney told me, "I think teachers could have realized that I wasn't engaging in the classroom. Like I wasn't raising my hand to like, give the answer all the time. I was just doing the bare minimum of what I needed to do and keeping my head down." A small change like this could have helped.

A while ago, during the job search that eventually landed me my current position, I realized that I greatly appreciated postings that were direct about deal-breaker level requirements, strongly encouraged credentials, and things that were "nice to have." For many of us, *assignments structured in this way – in hierarchies of necessity – would have gone a long way towards making it so we didn't have to try to read between the lines as much.*

Whitney described one of her common tactics for ensuring she grasped the assignment materials. "I was one that would, you know, find a teacher or two each year that I would try to become closer with just so that I could, you know, bounce things off of them after class," she said, "or have someone that I felt comfortable with if I didn't understand things." The problem is that it takes a lot of agency and, frankly, bravery to seek out a teacher, especially a new one. I am sure readers are already being very clear with their students that they can come to them if they have questions, but I do wonder how often this is reiterated throughout the year. If you told me in September and I breeze through the material until January, I don't think I'm coming to you with questions at that point – I'm just going to hold my breath and hope to survive. *So it's that frequent repetition, even or especially for students who don't "seem" to need space for questions, that will go a long way for us.*

Even what I've suggested here may not work for all of us. You may come across a student you are pretty sure is a neurodivergent person of color, and they may get annoyed at having information delivered in hierarchies, or they may find subtitles distracting. The final suggestion above, then, about repeating the existence of an open door to ask questions, ensure that there is space inside of that open door for students to think about and discuss the way they best process material, and allow them to offer changes that might help them. As you've already heard, many of us won't know we're neurodivergent at all just yet, so a lot of the work is going to be in teasing out what would help us feel heard long before we can articulate it. As the chapters continue, hopefully through all of the suggestions made, an environment can be created that would make it a lot less scary to speak up when we need support, but I won't pretend it'll be easy for you, or for us.

Note

1   https://my.clevelandclinic.org/health/symptoms/23154-neurodivergent

3

Getting Things Done

On Completing (and Not Completing) Assigned Tasks

Whatever clever title I want to use, this chapter is ultimately about "executive function," which is basically a fancy way to describe the ability to get things done. When I first learned about the concept, I was certain that I, like many neurodivergent people, would be described as having "poor" executive function, but the more time I spent thinking about it, and about my ability to, you know, do stuff, the more I realized it wasn't so much that I had "bad" executive function, but that its presence was entirely conditional, and that the gap between its presence and absence had had a massive impact on my life.

I would argue that, among all of the traits you'll learn about in this book, neurodivergent students' level of executive function is one of the most frustrating things about us. It's almost impossible for us not to demonstrate our skills in some way during a given school year, and when we're good, *we're good* – a neurodivergent person in their element is one of the most impressive things you'll ever see. And so, if our teachers notice us struggling but aren't aware of our conditions, they might see us excelling in certain circumstances and utterly floundering in others and assume that, in the latter situations, we are just not trying. This chapter isn't an excuse for all of those times per se, but, I hope, it can

DOI: 10.4324/9781003465126-4

serve as a bit of an explanation for why we sometimes just can't get it going, even though we are the most efficient students you'll ever meet at other times.

Counter-Narratives

I had a habit of waiting until the very last second to do my homework in seventh grade. Yes, seventh grade again – the year I had Mr. Rossi. Every weekend I would ignore my obligations until the very last minute and then do as much as I could on Sunday night. I rarely finished everything that was required of me, but I usually got enough done that I didn't have to get yelled at in *every* class on Mondays – only about half of the classes on average. It would have been significantly less stressful to just do my damn homework every weekend, especially because whenever I bothered to sit down and focus on it, it wasn't really very hard. But, for reasons I hope you'll all understand by the end of this chapter, that wasn't as easy as it might have seemed from an outside perspective, which is indeed the perspective that all of my teachers had. Why couldn't I just *do what they asked*, they wondered, especially because they knew that I was intellectually capable of it. My science teacher spent the entire year frustrated with my lack of effort and openly praised my classmates in comparison, and my English teacher, who clearly wanted me to just *try*, bent over backwards to get me to hand in my assignments despite every pathetic excuse I used when I didn't have my papers when I was supposed to. Later, in 12th grade, he was my teacher again in a class about screenwriting, and by that point I'd figured out how to push through my blocks and produce material, and he was one of the most encouraging educators I'd ever worked with. But in seventh grade? He was just as frustrated as everyone else.

If I'd told my family I had homework to do, they would have gladly cleared time and space for me to focus on what I needed to get done, but by seventh grade I was years into my habit of assuring everyone that I was on top of things and just ignoring Monday's impending doom. Usually I'd do at least some of my homework but, for whatever reason, towards the end of October that school year, I just didn't do a single thing I was assigned, and spent the weekend doing whatever I could to ignore how awful that Monday was sure to be. I managed not to think about my homework until we were approaching home after a weekend family trip, and even to this day I can remember how heavy the weight of what I was going to have to deal with the next day felt once I finally realized how much trouble I was going to be in. Did I do anything about it? No. I just went to sleep and woke up without any way of resolving the issue.

Around this time I'd started riding the subway to school by myself after my last babysitter had been let go. I'd memorized all the stops in the subway system when I was four, and so my parents trusted me to get myself to school even though I was only eleven. If you're outside of New York, that might well seem absurd, but I assure you there are plenty of kids who take public transportation to school unsupervised in middle school there, and we get to school more safely than kids who are driven. But of course, not all of these kids are panicking about the homework they haven't done, and so, on this particular Monday, my father got off the train near Wall Street as he usually did, and I rode a few extra stops into Brooklyn Heights and then, breathing heavily, just . . . didn't get off the train when I reached my school's stop.

For the next three days, I basically luxuriated in the nerdiest little rebellion I could have possibly had. Every day I'd bid goodbye to my parents and tell them I was going to school, and then I'd ride the subway all day, getting off around noon and using my lunch money to go to McDonald's, which was obviously the highlight of this whole endeavor. I came home around the same time I was expected, so I figured no one would be the wiser, and truth be told, it worked just fine for a while because my school didn't bother to call home until the end of that third day. I bring this whole story up not just because it was something of a meltdown I had when faced with a series of deadlines, but also because I'll never actually know whether my teachers didn't notice I wasn't in class or simply didn't care. I find it hard to believe that they would have been oblivious to the absence of their only Black student, a nuisance who spent most classes trying and failing to crack jokes, but, especially because my attendance was usually impeccable, maybe they just trusted me and my family. Either way, school figured it out eventually, and although the middle school administrator was patient and kind with me when I was forced to show up on the Thursday, they still never asked me what the problem was, and I went right back to gritting my teeth, holding my breath, and not getting much of anything done.

"What do I have?" Rose asked me when I inquired about her diagnosis. "I think it's a little bit complicated. But I guess I'll start with what I was initially diagnosed with. As a teenager, I was diagnosed with major depressive disorder and ADHD, predominantly inattentive, which I've pretty much always had the symptoms very, very clearly. I think over time, the mood disorder component of it has gotten a little bit more complicated. And I've been diagnosed with bipolar II.

"I think there's been some dispute among clinicians about what that mood disorder exactly is," she continued, "and whether or not I might have some sort of like, PTSD and kind of distinguishing difference between like bipolar versus PTSD and cyclothymia. But there's definitely a little more nuanced mood disorder component. So the only thing I'm really confident that I have is ADHD and mood disorder . . . Sorry, I forgot to name Social Anxiety Disorder. But I think there's some dispute about that."

Rose is a postdoc who was originally raised in California. Like Ellie, she has a doctorate in neuroscience. She received her first diagnosis in her late teens, but as described above, that was hardly the end of the story. "The material was very, very easy for me," she explained. "So I didn't really struggle on that front because it was so easy, but I quickly got to the point where I felt like school was a waste of time, like later in elementary school, like not being challenged at all and sort of trying to start to detach and I don't know, try to seek out other things that were stimulating and maybe start to get depressed. But I think how that really started to show up is just lots of procrastination. Like I couldn't do the work until it was the last minute. I couldn't get any motivation. Like that was what I had to depend on to get things done. And I still have that problem."

Procrastination descends from the Latin for "deferred to tomorrow," and it's a habit that's certainly not limited to neurodivergent students. Almost everyone I knew growing up told me about how often they waited until the last minute to do anything, and most of them seemed proud of the unnecessary pressure they'd put on themselves. I wasn't really one for procrastinating myself per se – I just didn't do things. But for most of the people I interviewed, deferring to tomorrow was their modus operandi. As Rose explained to me, though, "eventually it gets to the point where it's not sustainable."

She brought in other emotions that recurred across my interviews when I asked about executive function. "It starts to affect the quality, right?" she said. "I reflect on it sometimes and it just, it really feels like a lot of what I've been able to get done is really just some combination of fear, anxiety and procrastination. And once the fear and anxiety is gone, it's really hard to motivate myself to get things done that I don't care to do or I'm not stimulated."

Since it's rare that we are able to articulate this mix of emotions when trying to justify incomplete work, the fear and anxiety that contribute to our struggles with early completion get pushed out of the conversation, and all that remains is the perception of laziness and a lack of effort.

"I would say that in terms of completing tasks, I'm a procrastinator," said Robyn, an attorney from the DC/Maryland/ Virginia area in her mid-40s. "I would get things done but like at the very last minute and then it was not always the most positive situation.

"I definitely try to do too many tasks at the same time," she continued, "and would get distracted by you know, trying to clean my room, would lead to trying to organize something else."

We aren't unaware of our tendencies, though. Everyone I spoke to had developed some sort of technique to drag themselves over these constant hurdles. For Ellie, she gamified her task completion. "I think one of the things that I did as a child," she explained, "which is quite kind of funny to me now is I made up this game called the Goal Setting game. I was like 12 or 13 years old. It would be like the task you need to do, you set an amount of time and then you call a friend maybe on the phone, or there with you, and you say okay, I'm going to do exactly this much. And you can't do anything else during the time period. Can you just imagine a 12-year-old playing this cycle, after school every day to get my homework done?"

She was clear, though, that she rarely struggled to complete tasks if she could see a direct connection to a possible grade, and to the previously mentioned social approval she sought by performing well academically. "I wouldn't have task completion problems if I could see it tied to a grade," she said, "but I could struggle a lot to complete or totally avoid for a long, long time, something that's clerical." If you compare this to what Rose said about fear and anxiety, you can see a thread connecting the two, where without some powerful motivator beyond just the fact that something was required, it was an inordinate challenge for us to complete what was laid in front of us.

For my own part, I eventually learned to grab onto every emotion I could if I had a relatively dull task to complete. Fear? Sure. Anxiety? Always. Spite? What a powerful but ultimately destructive form of fuel! Rose found herself doing much the same thing. "I can definitely relate to that," she told me. "Spite carried me to the end of graduate school and now that's not really a sustainable motivation strategy." It'll burn you up from the inside, but if merely having a deadline isn't itself enough reason to get something done, you use whatever you can.

Rachel described having to create – or wait for – a sense of urgency to complete tasks. "I would often get my tasks done – I'm thinking again about high school – the period before the class because I needed that urgency. I absolutely needed urgency to get it done. And so I became really sneaky.

"And, you know, teachers of course, walk around the classroom," she explained, "so I have to be very careful about that. And it's not that I didn't want to pay attention or learn in that class. It's just that, you know, I put off the assignment the night before, because there wasn't that sense of urgency. So oftentimes, the sense of urgency when I was left to my own devices, so my parents helped me when I was in elementary school and all of that, but when I became older and was getting my homework done on my own, it would often look like doing it the day of and that followed me. That still follows me." Indeed, despite the fact that this book is chiefly concerned with our K-12 experiences, few of us have "outgrown" our younger habits entirely, for better or worse.

Terry related a pertinent example of how our tendency to wait until the last minute can collapse upon us when things go wrong. "Often I would procrastinate projects until the last minute," they said, "or, you know, do my homework the night before you know or a study for my exam or cram for my exam the night before. But I just again, like I always just posted because I was hyperlexic and hypercalcemic. So you know, high IQ kind of hides your neurodivergence for a long time."

They described how, despite having made it through a rigorous undergraduate experience, a master's program *and* a law degree, mostly using these same techniques, the onset of some serious health issues, along with logistical challenges, made it impossible to pull off the last-minute trick much longer. "When my professors saw me showing up for class not having read the material, not getting to class on time, not handing my papers on time, they saw this as a lack of commitment to the program," they told me. "Even though like this was my life. I was living my dream of like finally doing a PhD in psychological anthropology, focusing on the things that were of interest to me, but to the faculty it just looked like I was not committed. And in part they brought up the fact that I was like, I was in the Vagina Monologues while I was doing my PhD program. But really this is just part of the ADHD brain is that you need to be fully self-expressed in order to be functional."

I reiterate that although the focus here is on our younger years, my inclusion of our later experiences is meant to demonstrate that even if we don't crash and burn while we're in your classroom, the bomb is going to go off eventually, and it would be so much better for us if we could find the support to learn sustainably before it comes back to bite us. Also, Terry's final statement about being "fully self-expressed" is key, and recalls Rose's comment about stimulation, or a lack thereof, being a barrier. As we saw in Chapter 1 with Marie's story about tennis balls and the distance to the sun, what stimulates us is often not what we're required to do, and without that stimulation, we're either going to have to come up with a game like Ellie, use other emotions like Rose or like me, or just hope that waiting until the last minute doesn't lead to catastrophe.

Even when we do manage to get everything done, then, it often comes at the expense of mental stability. Marie detailed the cycle of pressure that has followed her from middle school up to the present day:

> I was never the kid that [my mother] had to harp on about doing homework or getting things done. But I definitely stressed myself out a lot. So it was to the point of intense perfectionism. And part of that was also coming from a low-income background knowing that if I didn't get scholarships, I wasn't going to college. Like that added a lot of pressure to my situation where it was like, 'Okay, I know that I need to get an A in this class because I need to keep this GPA because I need to get scholarships because of this.' This builds a ripple effect where I probably forced myself to grow up a little too fast in that sense, where I couldn't just enjoy high school, couldn't just enjoy middle school. I always felt that pressure to get good grades and succeed. And I think it became a hyper fixation, to be quite honest, especially in the classes that were really difficult for me. I was bad at math. So I decided that I would just take every math class that was offered to me at my tiny high school until I was good at math. So I took all the way up to AP calculus. And that was unnecessary. Nobody asked me to do that. Nobody made me take calculus and it wasn't required. I just forced myself to do it. Because I was determined to overcome being bad at math. And so I think half the time the reason that I finished tasks is because I let myself hyper fixate on them. And that carried on through college as well, half the time that I would be studying or doing an assignment, I would go to a coffee shop and sit there for hours and I wouldn't leave until it was done. And I mean,

I know that's how you get stuff done sometimes, but it was very deliberate and forced, I wasn't just casually working on my homework, like I was forcing myself to sit there and hyper fixate. And I realized now that most people don't actually have to do that. They can just go and do their homework for 30 minutes a day. They can do it, you know, work on paper for a couple hours a week and then have their paper done at the end of the semester. But it was never like that for me. It was like 'Okay, I'm gonna work on this paper for six hours and I'm going to get it done.' And that's how I'm going to work and it's been harder in my doctoral program to let myself have time to rest. Because I'm so used to this forceful hyper fixation cycle that I've been in.

Some of what she said here ties into a later chapter on lack of focus and hyperfocus, so I will leave some of it aside for the time being, but I wanted to include all of this directly from the source so you could see how the cycle builds upon itself and takes decades to escape. What happens to us as adolescents reverberates long after we're in a middle school classroom, to the point where we often don't know any other way of completing our obligations.

With all of this said, though, the people in this book are still examples of students who, you know, *figured it out* to some extent. We wouldn't have made it to college and, for almost all of us, to advanced degrees if we didn't find some way to get enough done to excel. I can understand in reading a book that centers on the most successful neurodivergent students of color if you might think that those of us with what one might call "low support needs" aren't really who we need to worry about. Like, yes, I obviously eventually started doing my homework, and in fact swung very far in the other direction by the time I got to 10th grade, doing as much of my homework as possible on my subway ride home and sitting in the station if I hadn't finished by the time I reached my destination – *and I missed my stop more than once*. Every so often I'd struggle again, but by the time I got to my doctoral program I was always weeks or months ahead of everyone else, and I was often frustrated when my classmates would ask for extensions on assignments I'd already handed in. From the outside, I made it look easy, but on the inside, I was deeply anxious, telling myself if I took my foot off the gas for just one second at any point, who's to say I wouldn't fall right back into the habits I had as a preteen, and so it was imperative I dive into everything immediately. Sure, I get a lot done and I get it done fast, and that's better than *not* getting it done, but I don't know that I've really been able to breathe for a long, long time, and at some point I should probably come up for air. Unfortunately, I've forgotten how.

Takeaways

"Why can't you just do it?"

This is the refrain so many of us heard. And the fact of the matter is, we mostly don't know nor can we articulate the answer to this question. When things line up for us, we can get just about anything done, but when they don't, we can flounder with little path to rescue. My hope with this chapter is to demonstrate that it is not a lack of effort that obstructs our progress but rather a lack of alignment. For the people featured in this book, we are positioned as "exceptional" students of color, intellectually distanced from our identities, and ambassadors for our race whether or not we were aware of such a status. For any neurodivergent student, not accomplishing an obligation might be seen as a personal failure, but for *us*, it was felt as a community failure. That wasn't necessarily enough to convince us to get everything done, but it was the weight hanging over us when we did or didn't do what we were supposed to. So how can you help us?

"Maybe there should be more snack times even when we're older," Rachel told me. "I know they have it for younger kids, but I feel like we're not allowed to have any sort of food. Or like if we could have granola bars or something I feel like that would be really helpful." You might laugh thinking about late-adolescent snack time, but remember that we all had to call upon whatever emotional reserves we could find to get through the tasks that had been assigned to us.

Marie told me that all she wanted from her teachers was grace. There's a trend where people are arguing that all deadlines should be abolished, but not only is that impractical, it's also, as you can see from the narratives above, not what would help us – if we didn't have boundaries at all, we might never get anything done in a class we didn't love. But for us, *what we needed was grace, or, more accurately, the signal that we should – and could – give grace to ourselves.* Without that intense feeling that we needed to beat ourselves up for all perceived failures, who knows if we would have achieved as much as we have, but I am pretty sure that it would have been worth the risk to try.

Ellie told me that her friends had gone a long way towards ensuring she was never fully adrift. "I think I again was looking for that like social approval and I think that grades were really manifesting that," she said, "and I think also grades were my way of showing that I wasn't okay. Despite difficult things that were going on in my life, I think almost performing academically well is a way of masking." Her peers did what they could but they aren't trained to provide the professional support needed. With that said, *actively constructing a buddy/pair system could go a long way towards helping people avoid falling into the stressful mental traps that are common to us neurodivergent folks.* Even if the students roll their eyes when given a "buddy," the ones that benefit will appreciate the effort in time. Indeed, I spend far too much of my free time in a Discord server with fellow academic types, and given that the forum is overindexed with us neurodivergent folks, it's useful to note that pairing up to be accountable for work is something that is popular and helpful.

Finally, I was going to mention that we ought to receive some measure of agency in our academic obligations, but then I realized that merely getting to choose might just send us off into the intellectual wilderness. I think about an administrator from my high school who sat with me at the beginning of 10th grade and told me my verbal scores on standardized tests weren't great. We had talked about what I enjoyed reading, and truth be told, I didn't do much pleasure reading at all between fourth grade and 10th. She told me, and this is the key, that if I found something I loved to consume, I could use my enthusiasm for it to power through my academic obligations. Every school sends out summer reading lists – and I always ignored mine – but it wasn't until she made the point that my fun could be tied into my obligations that it all clicked for me. As it turned out, I ended up reading a lot of Stephen King novels, and she laughed and told me it wasn't exactly what she'd hoped for, but she told me to keep going, and it was certainly true that if I could read a thousand pages of *The Stand*, I could probably handle whatever I was told to read. I would also be lying if I didn't admit that, despite what the author has revealed herself to be, the Harry Potter series helped remind me I enjoyed reading. My parents even got mad at me for refusing to put down *The Order of the Phoenix* on one of our vacations – in my defense, that book is approximately 875,000 pages long, and Sirius Black dies! (*Okay, it's 875 pages. And, uh, spoiler alert for a 20-year-old book. You've had enough time.*) The point I'm making isn't just to allow neurodivergent students to read for pleasure so much as to explicitly connect external pleasures to our assignments. With that bridge, we can get so much more done than we'd ever otherwise expect, and so I hope that this section helps readers understand that we very much want to get things done, regardless of how much it might seem that we don't care.

4

Coloring Outside the Lines
On Doing Things Our Own Way

One of the most important things I've learned from the work of Paolo Freire is a rejection of what he refers to as the "banking" method of pedagogy. He described it accordingly:

> Education . . . becomes an act of depositing, in which the students are depositories and the teacher is the depositor. Instead of communicating, the teacher issues communiqués and makes deposits which the students patiently receive, memorize and repeat. This is the 'banking' concept of education, in which the scope of action allowed to the students extends only as far as receiving, filing and storing the deposits.[1]

My understanding of this is that educators are positioned as the only true experts in the room, with students being positioned as lacking insight and information that can thus only be provided by the person in front of the chalkboard. Anyone reading this will know this isn't the case – all of our students are experts on themselves, even if they need support in absorbing the new material. But I do think that, for neurodivergent students in particular, there is a fierce resistance to being treated as depositories, and so

DOI: 10.4324/9781003465126-5

we tend not to go along with all of the requirements in assigned work if they don't make intuitive sense to us, which often places us in opposition to what our teachers and schools would prefer. Too much of teacher training still prepares educators to see students as places into which academic deposits can be made, to the point that even well-meaning teachers still retain the muscle memory of their students being positioned as voids to be filled. Indeed, I can't pretend I didn't ascribe to this ideology in my early teaching days, and part of why I write about education now is to try and atone for this wrongheaded approach. But ultimately, the issue at hand is that, no matter what you believe, neurodivergent students aren't going to go along with being positioned as empty vessels.

Counter-Narratives

I never learned how to type "properly." Don't get me wrong, I know how to use a keyboard and I bang words out really fast, but the traditional way you're supposed to lay your fingers across the keys? I can't do it. They tried to teach me, the way I'm sure they tried to teach you, but it became a battle I was determined to win, and, given that I am still a hunt-and-peck typist to this day, I'm not sure I "won," but in the moment, it felt like a triumph.

We're talking about third grade now, a time before schools had easy access to the internet or any sort of sophisticated technology set-up. There was this game they had us playing, which the current internet tells me was called *Type! – how clever! –* where you were given sentences and were tasked with typing it out both quickly and accurately. You were also responsible for controlling a little black-and-white hurdler, and he would run faster if you typed faster, but he'd fall down every time you made an error. I'm sure some of you who are around my age can recall this game. We were taught the rules and had our hands placed on the right keys and then they'd have us compete, presumably with the idea that gamifying typing would help us forget we were actually being taught. If you're a lot younger than I am and a digital native I'm sure this all sounds absurd to you but schools didn't really know How To Computer back then, so this was state-of-the-art technological pedagogy right there.

Anyway, so at first I did terribly at the game because it was physically uncomfortable for me to hold my fingers in the "correct" positions. I could do it, briefly, but I'd have to concentrate so hard on doing so that I'd still make countless mistakes, more or less the same pattern that I follow when I have to make sustained eye contact. Now, I did like video games as a kid, and spent a lot of time in my bedroom making up imaginary athletes that were, in contrast to my own talents, actually good at sports, but most of the time I was actually pretty bad at the games themselves, to the point where by the time I got to college people would ask me to play *Halo* because they knew they could beat me. I have pretty terrible spatial awareness, so anything that is more complex than running in a straight line was something I struggled with, even if it's just on a screen. But this *Type!* game? It was (virtually) running in a straight line! And as much as my teachers told me that the point was to balance speed and accuracy, I also figured out pretty quickly that the game wasn't exactly sophisticated enough to prevent me from winning even if my little avatar fell on his face a bunch of times. Every mistake I made, I'd lose a few milliseconds of speed, but if I was otherwise just that much faster, I'd still come out ahead. So that's exactly what I did.

My teachers were frustrated because I was rejecting what they considered to be the point of the lesson, but I protested that, if I was winning, it didn't really matter how I got to the finish, so long as I wasn't cheating. What was the point of making the little man on the screen stay upright if I came in second? Eventually they just gave up and wrote about it in my report card, where I'd already gained a reputation for an inability to, both literally and metaphorically, color inside the lines. Would I be better off if I set my fingers on the keyboard "correctly?" Maybe. But I knew how to get the words onto the screen, so I figured it didn't matter how I went about doing so. This of course is a pretty stubborn way for a seven-year-old to behave, but for folks like us, if it doesn't make sense or doesn't feel right, we're probably just not going to do it, much of a problem as that often presents for us in classroom settings.

On a closely related note, but conveyed in more academic verbiage, neurodivergent folks have been shown to display a higher *justice sensitivity* than their peers.[2] You can read the cited article if you would like considerably more detail, but how it relates to me and my refusal to type with my fingers on the "appropriate" letters is that we find it very difficult, almost impossible, to just go along with things that we perceive to be unfair or even just uncomfortable. Sometimes that involves broader societal injustices, and sometimes it's as seemingly small as knowing that you're completing the assignment well enough by doing it your own way and refusing to go through the motions just because you're told to do so.

An ADHD coach named Jacqueline Sinfield put it this way:

> ADHDers don't follow arbitrary rules; just rules that make sense to them. If there is a rule that prevents fairness, then a person with ADHD is more than happy to break it. At an airport, imagine there are long lines at the check-in counter for coach class. Yet the business class line could be empty. Many people with ADHD would take their coach ticket and try to check-in in the business line, because it makes no logical sense to stand and wait in line. This same principle is applied to all situations that don't seem fair.[3]

Unfortunately, a lot of school is, in fact, going through the motions because you're told to do so; in the example used by Sinfield, there are a lot of airport lines you have to stand in while staring at empty nearby lines. Therein lies the tension and the struggle for us and our teachers. And yes, I do hate airplane boarding procedures, why do you ask?

This fairness orientation can also leave us even more isolated from our peers. Rose told me about her frequent confusion at the way things were "supposed" to be and the impact this had on her overall trajectory.

Not really understanding why social structures are the way they are, why people are communicating the way they are. It's like a lot of kind of trying to analyze patterns and figure out like, "Okay, how is this person supposed to be," copying or testing different models on it, and then it's like, "Okay, well, I did it wrong again." I feel like it was a lot of like, trying to guess how a person is supposed to operate based on what I saw around me. Which I think sometimes led to trouble, a lot of emotional distress, a lot of identity issues, a lot of things that detracted from academics that have nothing to do with the academics at all. There's not a lot of social reward associated with being a nerd or somebody who's very compassionate or justice oriented, someone who for example really cares about saving the trees. I remember giving a speech, or [being in] a speech contest about deforestation; those are the things I really cared about, but they were not helping my social persona. And so I think there was a point where I started to detach a lot from performing well academically, because it just made me seem more weird or like a teacher's pet, or I don't know, I feel like and have always felt like people get mad at me for those things. Or there's more social projections associated with doing well. And so it's like, it doesn't matter whether you're doing horrible or you're doing amazing, people are still going to hate me for it and it's super confusing.

Sometimes it's social justice, and then sometimes it's just the way you're supposed to complete your work. Marie told me about her mental process when given assignments. "When I am told to do something one specific way, but a question comes up along the way, I want to know how much I can push the envelope," she said. "You know, how strictly do I have to do this the way that you said, you know, so I felt like that was a struggle I can think of. I took chemistry in high school and some of it was very straightforward. Some of it wasn't but I always wanted to know why, or what or how, and sometimes there wasn't room for those questions to be asked."

Robyn echoed the idea that she wasn't likely to cheat or be unethical – which one would hope for an attorney – but would find her own way to the finish line within acceptable boundaries. "I'm pretty specific and literal," she said. "I mean, I think in that if I felt there was wiggle room in the rules, I'm comfortable exploring the gray area, but it has to be something that I can argue as being within the rules, if that makes sense."

Rose has started to see a repeated pattern now that her own young son is old enough to receive homework. "I think there were often times when I tried to do it my own way," she explained. "Like, sometimes the instructions didn't really make any sense particularly with things like math. And I actually noticed that with my own son, like they're trying to force you to do it in a very specific way. And that's just not the most intuitive way in my head or his head. There's like this obsession with showing the work, but there are other ways to get to the answer."

"Show your work" is a command that makes sense in the abstract, but one that still rankles when instructions are unclear or seemingly contradictory. Oftentimes, especially in math or other quantitative classes, we'd be told both that the final answer was the most important, but also that the steps we took were the real lesson we needed to learn. It depends on the subject whether or not the steps should be weighted as heavily in assessment as the final result. In geometry, where much of the purpose is detailed, step-by-step proofs based in logic, yeah, you probably can't skip any steps, and let me tell you I sure was bad at geometry – *you probably also need better spatial awareness for that*. In elementary school, though, when tasked with multiplication and division, I usually quickly did the math in my head and wrote the answer down, and it sure always seemed like they just didn't believe I could be capable of such things. It's different now that there are smartphones available, so, yes, it's easier to cheat in theory – I didn't even own a calculator until I was required to purchase one for Algebra – but I am already dreading the possibility of having to help my own son with Common Core math or something of the sort, because I'm sure I'll be able to see the answer and struggle to explain to him why the steps are just as important. At heart, I know I'll just tell him he has to do it because it's what schools require and we'll muddle our way through it so he doesn't get assessed poorly, but if the way his brain works as a toddler is any indicator, he'll be doing it in his head all the same.

"At this point, particularly, we're talking about like, high school or before because so much happened and there's kind of a lot of a blur there," Rose continued. "And since I didn't finish high school, eventually got to the point where it's like, I'm not actually doing the work anymore." This conflict between coloring inside and outside of the lines isn't just a trivial concern – for us, we can often feel as though we're being punished not for misunderstanding the material or even not putting in effort, but just because we don't fit the expectations, and there's a non-zero chance we can check out or give up entirely.

"Always with math," Rachel told me, "I would get the answer and I didn't show the work the way they wanted me to show the work. Yep, and I gotta imagine that still a problem today in K through 12, that we're expecting kids to show the work a certain way. Or we assume they're cheating and I think we need to give kids more credit than that."

Whitney concurred. "I would do minimal showing work on something. But I'm like, but I swear I did it," she said. "It's interesting, because it's like, our processing is so much faster. So I'm understanding the thing, but I don't always understand how to *get* to the thing, right? It's like it's clicking and I'm like, 'Ah, got it,' but how do I get to the thing without you, like you said, making me feel like I'm slow or not understanding the material."

As Terry mentioned a few chapters back, plenty of us, despite sometimes receiving poor assessment in these sorts of classes because of all this, are hypercalcemic, i.e., particularly skilled with numbers. Indeed it's something of a stereotype for neurodivergent people, if you can think about any pop culture representation of our community, even the ones that mostly make us look like aliens – such as Sheldon Cooper of *The Big Bang Theory* and *Young Sheldon*. (*I know he is not actually tagged with a diagnosis, and that he's painted as a "genius," but he is more or less unable to function outside of his specific interests.*) "It depends on if it makes sense to me," Terry explained. "And then I can do it the way they say but if it doesn't make sense to me then I'm probably going to do it in the order that makes more sense to me, or I'm going to do it but only because it comes with a point. Right? So one example would be when you have to show your work doing math, right? I do a lot of it in my head, but they want to see the steps so I write out the steps for them. But if I'm practicing on my own, I'm not writing off the steps while I'm practicing."

"If it makes sense to me" is probably the mantra of this entire chapter. As adults, we can protest or ask questions when obligations don't line up with the way we'd be best served, but as children, and particularly younger children, we're unlikely to be able to articulate this, and instead end up, say, mashing keyboard buttons to win a typing race. Or, as Whitney explained, we might put a great deal of effort into trying to follow the rules, but in the process spend considerable extra time doing so. She described her experience like this:

> As a really young child, I was always very much a rule follower. And I think that was to do a lot with that I grew up in a really turbulent, unstable household as well. So you know, I was always a little nervous to, how do I say, bring more attention to myself just because our household was so chaotic and things were really unstable. I say all that because that affected how I was as a student, right? Like I didn't want to bring any more attention to myself and the issues I had going on. I'm the oldest child too, so I was also hyper aware of how my actions could impact the household or that's how I felt. So I would do the assignments and do the work, how it had to be done, but I would spend extra time reading the chapter from front to back to like, understand what I was supposed to be doing, or, you know, researching on the computer, getting examples from the internet.

The community pressure I mentioned in the previous chapter is something that can't be ignored when discussing neurodivergent students of color in particular. Even if you haven't been informed that a student's home life is especially turbulent the way Whitney's was, struggling to contend with our ways of thinking being challenged and dismissed while also dealing with what it's like to walk through the world in our bodies is a very heavy cognitive load, heavier than what most children should have to shoulder, especially when we're likely not to have the support of a diagnosis or any codified treatment.

Ellie also mentioned pressures from her home life and how she dealt with them. "I think I felt like I was a pretty self confident little kid," she said. "Another thing was, I have an older brother who has ADHD and I think, a lot of attention for the family and because of him in the family, grades were really de-emphasized because he got terrible grades. And so I think like, they didn't want to put too much emphasis on self-worth with grades. But nonetheless, therefore, I was like, much better than my brother's [grades] were, and I think competitiveness fits that game thing to have, like trying to be, you know, beating my brother's.

"I got the instruction for my older brothers that we shouldn't let other people know the problems in our family," she added. "A lot of things were supposed to be secrets and also a lot of things were secrets like *from* my family if I would be not perfect in some way."

The more of these stories I share, the more I realize it's somewhat remarkable that all of us did graduate and succeed by most metrics. And as much as I'd love to sit here and proclaim that our unique ways of approaching assignments are unimpeachable, this really can come back to bite us and derail our ambitions if we're not lucky.

By the time I got to high school, I was almost a decade removed from my years as a precocious little multiplication and division boy, and math had become a lot more abstract. As I mentioned, I was bad at geometry, and then in Algebra 2 I was confounded by the concept of an asymptote – "what do you mean it just approaches the line and never actually reaches it?" – and it just kept getting worse and worse in each successive year, until I was spending entire Sunday afternoons staring at my math homework, unable to admit to myself I didn't understand a subject that had always come easily to me. Because of my prior reputation, when I handed in math homework unfinished, long after the years where I didn't actually do my assignments, teachers often thought I just wasn't putting any effort in, which somehow was always the conclusion people drew no matter what I did. And so, especially as students of color who are categorized as exceptions in many ways, it can be nearly impossible to ask for this sort of support, before even considering the time we'd spent trying to demonstrate that our unique approach could be just as effective. So the challenge then becomes, how do you support someone who can't fit inside the box when, sometimes, the box is all there is?

Takeaways

This is definitely a tricky set of items to try and juggle. If you don't come up with some sort of rubric or an equivalent, not only might your assessments be seen as too subjective, but also it's going to take you a millennium to complete your grading, and as much as I can tell you that it would be nice if we could move away from letter grades, assessment isn't going anywhere, so there's going to have to be some sort of standard. The key is to try and avoid prescriptive expectations as much as possible.

When I was a novice teacher in South Korea, the first time I think I really connected with a group of students was by coming up with a group project where they got to design their own countries, complete with laws, flags, cultures, and so forth. Standardized testing may feel onerous here in the States, but it doesn't compare to how much pressure exists over there,[4] so I wanted to give my students a chance to learn in a way that allowed them to feel creative and yet still use the English we had been practicing. The success of this project and the joy it inspired is one of the reasons I decided to make a go of an education career after I came home.

What I tell my young adult students now – *I wonder if you all forgot that I still do teach, even if it's college and grad students* – is that all I want to see is some evidence they are engaging with the material and have taken lessons away from the class. I offer them several options for how they can submit assignments – could be an essay, a video presentation, even a podcast. Do they want to do it in groups or solo? I leave it to them. This isn't necessarily realistic for very young children, especially if you've been tasked with instilling basic academic procedures in them, but my point is that, *whatever rules you yourself have been required to follow, find whatever daylight is within them to let your students approach the assignments with as much freedom as you can reasonably allow.* I don't know for sure that my students – many of whom are students of color – are neurodivergent unless they tell me, but they always rate my approach highly, and were I still teaching high school, that would be the balance I would put much of my effort into pursuing.

Rachel echoed this sentiment when I asked what had worked for her. "I definitely have that outside of the box thinking," she said. "And so the teachers that really respected that were the ones where their assignments were not as prescriptive. They were really good at making the assignments. You know, get out what they wanted, but not make it overly prescriptive so that I wasn't able to be creative."

If you remember Marie's story about the tennis balls from Chapter 1, that's another example of coloring outside the lines in a way that enhances the direct lesson. Indeed, *it's clearly not the case that we should be able to simply ignore our assignments altogether, but helping us find the approach that might help us reach the answers instead of just assessing how closely we can follow a script would have gone a long way towards supporting us and preventing us from a lot of the pain we experienced.* It's a very tough math equation to figure out though, and, ironically, you're definitely going to have to show your work.

Notes

1   Freire, P. (1968, 3rd edition 1996) *Pedagogy of the Oppressed*. London: Penguin Books.
2   Bondü, R., and Esser, G. (2015) Justice and Rejection Sensitivity in Children and Adolescents with ADHD Symptoms. *European Child & Adolescent Psychiatry* 24(2), 185–198. doi:10.1007/s00787-014-0560-9. Epub 2014 May 31. PMID: 24878677.
3   https://untappedbrilliance.com/adhd-and-an-unusual-sense-of-fairness/
4   See the BBC article "Suneung: The Day Silence Falls Over South Korea" (https://www.bbc.com/news/world-asia-46181240) for more.

5

Remembering and Forgetting

On Having the Best and Worst Memory at the Same Time

So even if you are relatively unfamiliar with neurodivergent folks, this chapter's topic is probably one where you already know we operate differently from other people. You may or may not have known, for example, that we communicate differently from other people, or what executive function is, but you definitely could have guessed we have trouble with certain types of memory. Now, memory is a tricky beast, and an unreliable one at that. It's a risk to base most of this book on our memories as there are some, including those who've read my work before, who discount anything that is not seen as purely objective, whatever that is supposed to mean. But, as I've already written above, our experiences were shaped by how we were perceived, as is true of everyone, and so, imperfectly objective though these memories may be, I still do think that our attempts to correct the narrative have value, especially given the paucity of respectful research about us that isn't just about diagnostic disparities.

Let's take another brief history tour, helpfully provided by Nelson Cowan.[1] For convenience's sake, I'll most likely be using "working" and "long-term" memory throughout the remainder of

DOI: 10.4324/9781003465126-6

the chapter, but scholars and researchers have used a variety of terms to make these distinctions over the past century or so. For a time the binary was "primary" vs "secondary" memory, and the gradual evolution into using "short-term," "long-term," and "working" was mostly related to measuring dysfunction or decay. As ever, Something Being Wrong is often the driver of diagnosis and discourse, and for us, while people may praise us when one aspect of our memory (usually long-term) proves exceptional, we all have stories of where our working memory failed us. Unfortunately, because school tends to require both – and with technological advances making long-term memory slightly less central to academic success – when we demonstrate an aptitude for remembering very specific facts and figures that interest us but can't remember where we put our papers (or, in more recent years, where we saved a file), it's this that our educators have seized on, and it's this that is the source of our conflict. Without looking it up, I can tell you how many stations are in the NYC subway system – *It was 468 for most of my life but then they added Hudson Yards (469) and the Second Avenue stops so now it's 472, as of this writing* – but I have to add "lunch" to my calendar so I can get three separate reminders (phone vibration, and separate emails to phone and computer) or else I'll let the whole hour pass working on this chapter and then I won't have time to eat. Speaking of which, after I come back from the lunch break I've just been reminded of, I will tell you about how this discrepancy between long-term and working memory has impacted us in the classroom, how this is undoubtedly frustrating to our teachers, and how it's even more frustrating for us not to be able to "fix" the problem no matter how hard we try.

Counter-Narratives

Stop me if you've heard this before, perhaps just a few pages ago, but in middle school I had a teacher who singled me out for exhibiting a neurodivergent trait. But whereas Mr. O'Donnell and Mr. Rossi were well known for being tough teachers, Mr. Christopher was a Cool Teacher. You know the type. Maybe you're one yourself. He was young, he made up funny voices, and, aside from all that silliness, he used his generally goofy nature to be an effective educator most of the time. He wrote up mnemonic devices to help us remember both English and Latin grammar and to this day I can easily recall some of those jingles. Here's a snippet of one:

Demonstratives – **this, that, these** and **those!**
Possessives – take **your** hand off **my** nose!

That song, by the way, was set to the rhythm of the Beastie Boys' "Paul Revere," which was fairly recent at the time, and that group was extra popular at my school because a couple of them had briefly attended decades earlier. So, you know, Cool Teacher. Silly class, a lot of laughter, and most of us seemed to absorb the material effectively. This wasn't a Mr. Rossi situation where I just couldn't keep up – I really loved his class, and I had him two years in a row. I cheered when I got my schedule for eighth grade and it said "Latin – Christopher." Which is what makes this next story all the more upsetting in retrospect.

I had – and continue to have – a habit of not having the mental capacity to deal with large amounts of paper that I need to hold onto. These days I shove them into a drawer to deal with at a later time, which is not ideal when you actually need to find important papers. As an adult-diagnosed ADHD writer described them, "A junk drawer, a paperwork pile, a catch-all box in my hallway that holds items ranging in importance from troll dolls to gas bills."[2] People tend to call these places "doom boxes," which is apparently actually an acronym for "**d**idn't **o**rganize, **o**nly **m**oved." Funny. But anyway, when I was 12, the only "important papers" I was responsible for was my homework, and the only "doom box" in my possession was my giant, overflowing back-pack, a bottomless pit into which many important documents went to die. The sad thing is that, by this point, I was well aware of this issue and was no longer just Not Doing Homework.

The subway meltdown the previous year had in fact scared me straight to some extent, but I still couldn't get out of my own way.

On a particular Wednesday – *I told you my long-term memory was sharp* – Mr. Christopher asked everyone to pull out whatever folders we were using to organize our work, and everyone pulled out some shiny, colorful item. Because it was still better than losing everything, I pulled out my giant, fraying, overflowing folder and held it up triumphantly, proud I actually had *some* system of organization. Mr. Christopher stared at me and asked, sitting on the front of his desk like a Cool Teacher, if I really thought that was supposed to be an effective strategy. "That is totally bogus," he said, and I'm not sure what it is with teachers and attaching epithets to me, but thankfully no one on earth uses "bogus" as an insult so that was only humiliating for other reasons. Woohoo!

More seriously though, for this to happen from a teacher who was otherwise very fun was pretty heartbreaking. It's one thing for a stern teacher to be overly stern, but to be singled out for opprobrium by someone who is normally jovial was a much starker contrast than other such situations. I tried not to think about it for the time being, but the next year I was relieved not to see his name on my schedule.

I want to reiterate that I continue to believe that readers know they wouldn't behave the same way and so may not see much of a lesson in these narratives, but almost all of us have been through it at some point, and are probably bringing that experience into your classroom. When you're unfairly criticized for something you largely can't control, such as the way we fight against the limits of our working memory, it just becomes mounting evidence of your lack of worth, and that's a hard self-assessment to shake.

People had a lot to say about this one.

Rachel gave her take on what was truly being asked of her. "I'd have to reread something I just read over and over again to get it," she said, "and I think about history class or something like that. Where there's questions at the end of chapters, and it's all based on what you just read. And so I would often have to go back and reread even though I have, by all accounts, an easy time with reading comprehension. It's just, you may have lost me because I got bored. And so it really plays into my short-term memory, and if I'm able to remember it, so it involves a lot of rereading. And I just think about all of those assignments where we had to answer questions at the end of chapters and that just feeling very tedious to me." She's started to underline part of why this might be such a struggle for us, though I caution readers not to interpret our brains' assessment of a task as tedious to mean we are callous and uncaring – we don't have conscious control of these decisions our brains make.

"I have the short-term memory of a goldfish," Whitney told me. "So I will forget literally anything that I don't write down or put a reminder in my calendar or text myself so that I can remember to do that when I get to the store."

It has been said that there is something of a "tax" to being neurodivergent. Whether it's the particular struggles that come with a condition like autism[3] or the financial impulsiveness and memory issues more common to ADHD,[4] it costs considerable money to live inside of our brains, and I would hope I don't need to explain to readers how racism can compound a lack of financial stability. But in the moment, it mostly just feels like there's a hole in our heads where important information goes, never to be heard from again, and there's almost no way to retrieve it.

How has this tax cost me? Well, for one, I didn't double-check the vaccine-verification requirements on what would have been my son's very first plane trip in 2022 and had to reschedule an entire vacation . . . after being ready to board the flight at the gate. (*We had our shots, but we hadn't filled out the form the country required.*) Back when I was truly in immediate need of cash, I somehow threw away the check that contained my IRS tax refund and had to request a replacement. And when it comes to school, in the time before I started doing everything so early I couldn't possibly miss an assignment, I frequently forgot what I was told to do, even when I really tried. This meant I had to walk into class with the same shame I'd had when I hadn't bothered to do my work, and my teachers had no idea there was any difference in how much effort I'd put in.

These issues don't simply end when we graduate of course. As Rachel explained, "I buy groceries and they go bad because

I forgot that they exist." But when it comes to school, the tax is more akin to the way that teachers assumed we truly didn't care. "I found myself having to go back and ask 'what exactly did you mean' or 'what am I supposed to do now that I completed step one, I know you had three other steps, I don't remember what they are,'" Marie said. "And sometimes it was viewed as, 'well, you weren't listening.' And it's like, 'I'm listening. I assure you, I was listening.' But I just don't retain that information very well. You know, it's not a matter of me not engaging or me just shutting down and not paying attention when you're talking. It's a matter of, I heard you, and it literally did not stay in my brain.

"And I hated when I would be told I wasn't listening," she added, "because I was always listening. It just was a matter of me being able to retain it."

We do what we can – the interviewees told me about planners and alarms and all sorts of tactics – but ultimately, if the information wants to leave our brains, it will. On top of this, the pattern of being put on the spot doesn't help our ability to access whatever working memory we may possess. As Rose told me, "I think there's always been a lot of stress, really, at every level to me about being called out to speak or to perform in some way, in part just because of the way that I communicate and just the amount of like, social rejection that I've dealt with, it's just very anxiety provoking. Stressful."

Ellie told me about some of her familiar struggles with losing track of both items and time:

I definitely was always forgetting things. Leave my back-pack on the bus, late to the bus. My mom was a single mom from like, eight onwards, and I would have to call the neighbor, because my mom would be at work, to take me to school. I would be losing papers, I definitely struggled with that. I think nowadays with technology maybe some things can be easier like you know, you would have assignments and if you lose sight of that, like there's no just printing it out again.

In a way, technological advances have been a boon for folks like us, but on the other hand, there's also the possibility that they just allow us to mask our struggles more effectively and for a longer period of time.

"Long-term memory impeccable," Robyn said. "Won't remember people's names that I'm introduced to at a party, or meeting new people on a work team. It may take me a minute to remember who, what, what people's names are, but like, in terms of details, I remember the details of what was said in a meeting. If I wrote it down, I can probably remember, you know, pretty accurately where in my notebook or which notebook it's in, going back, you know, more than ten years of work. I'm definitely like a Rolodex of information for, like you said, trivia, useless tidbits of things. I remember my elementary school, or my DC public school ID number, which was obviously, you know, a long time ago, but don't remember the people who were on a panel with me last week, so I had to look it up. I would have to look it up."

I want to hone in on one thing Robyn said there, the "useless tidbits" part. Now, she said that because I'd used the word during our interview, but it's been a recurring theme through most of our lives. It's a nice party trick that we can perform the role of personified encyclopedia, but, if you think back to the introduction and the way our societal ideas have shaped our treatment, long-term memory isn't considered to be nearly as, shall we say, productive as the working memory that interferes with our daily obligations. We might be experts at long-term recall and pattern recognition, and, for many of us, this might be enough to carry us across the finish line of required standardized testing, but when you're teaching us, all you might see is someone who can tell you the capital of every country in the world but not what they had to do for homework the night before, and without the narratives that you're reading in this book, you might see that person as someone who just doesn't care about learning, which is very far from the truth. I'm taking a moment to make these points because just repeating the fact that we struggle with working memory is not much of a finding in itself – you probably know that. The argument I'd like to advance is that what our brains excel at is undervalued by our institutions and many of our educators, and we're often explicitly told as much.

Sometimes what we choose to study is dictated by these neurological patterns. Indeed, the fact that many of us excel at lower-level math is likely because of its predictability and the way it can be unlocked through deductive reasoning. Terry told me about how their memory shaped their academic focus:

> I mostly did math, physics, and then some more math, because you can figure out math. You can figure out processes, you start from your fundamentals. You do these things over and over again. And you learn how to figure things out. And so math and physics came really, I wouldn't say easily to me, math definitely came easily. To me physics was more difficult, but at least you could sort of figure those things out . . . I can't remember any historical dates. I can cram for the test and I can remember it long enough to pass the test. But once the test is over, none of the factual things stay in my head. And that's like, in addition to the things like losing my keys all the time, although I didn't have any keys in high school. But like losing common items, you know, losing common items or forgetting to do my chores or forgetting my homework. I forgot my homework almost every day. My mother thought I just didn't want to do my homework. But really I just didn't have the skills to pause at the end of the day and put what I needed for my homework into my bag. So that just wasn't a skill that I had and no one taught that to me because they just assumed that the reason that I was forgetting my homework was inten-tional. So now I do things like everything goes into my calendar – as you saw I almost forgot about our meeting today. Everything I have goes into my calendar and my items. I have specific places where my items live, you know, have a special bag that my keys go into or a spe-cial location in my house where I always put them and it has to be the place where I put them. What I mean is

I have to fail a few times and then find my item in that location. And then that becomes the location where I put it because that's where I put it. Does that make sense?

Absolutely! But it's extremely hard to articulate to a teacher when you're already anxious about letting them down.

I had a French teacher named Madame Laurent. She mostly liked me and wrote positively about me in my report cards, but she was definitely just as irked by me as a lot of my teachers. At the same time, I had a good friend named, let's just say, Kenny. Now I have no idea whether or not Kenny, who was definitely white, had any sort of neurodivergence going on. As far as I can tell, he was what a lot of my teachers thought I was, a kid who really didn't care that much about school, because his family was very important in the institution's infrastructure. All I know is that he had a habit of losing his papers that was just as pronounced as mine. The difference was, when he'd show up and admit he'd misplaced his work, she would sit with him and ask aloud, "Now Kenny, where did we put the assignment? Here in the folder?" And then, there it would be, and she'd ask him to remember it next time, even though we all knew she'd be right back to reminding him again. I certainly don't think that the way she supported him was bad, but I'm certain I only remember that it happened because no one ever took the time to help ensure I didn't lose anything, not before my graduate programs at least.

There are systems that can be created – as I said before, I use my phone and two email alerts for everything now, and, like Terry, I need to keep everything in exactly the same place if I ever want to see it again. As Terry told me about the way they have to live these days:

> Everything I own is in clear plastic tubs. That's how I store my items. I don't really have external storage that isn't clear. Because if I can't see it, it's gone. And, you know, it's like it's the same thing for directions. Even though I have lived in [California city] for several years now, I still can't find my way around without my GPS. It took me probably five years to get used to driving in

San Diego to where I knew how to find my way around to most places. And now that I've been gone from San Diego for, let's see, since the end of 2012, I can't find my way around San Diego anymore. I've spent a lot of time in Las Vegas driving around and I can't find my way around. It's brutal.

We all figured it out, as I've said and will keep saying. But all of these habits we had to create for ourselves, years or even decades after our teachers told us that the best we could do with our memory wasn't nearly good enough for them.

Takeaways

The good thing about us being examples of people who still encounter these challenges on a daily basis but have mostly fought them to a draw – much as we'd like them to, they're never going to go away – is that we do have guidance for how teachers can support students who exhibit these traits. And again, not just a student who appears to be forgetful or absent-minded, but one who displays both this struggle and impeccable skill in other forms of memory.

"I do remember us getting some type of planner book starting in middle school," Whitney said. "And that's really when I started kind of realizing that could be helpful, writing things down so that I wouldn't forget them." She says that extracurricular activities, in particular a sorority she joined in college, helped re-instill the value of these habits to the point where she's able to rely upon them to this day. This doesn't mean the short-term memory is stronger but that she has built enough of a habit to document what needs to be done before it disappears into the mental ether. Giving out planners or the virtual versions of them is nice, and schools should continue to do that, but *I contend that an explicit segment of an early section of every school year should be devoted to building these habits, for all students, and possibly in every different class subject, as organization looks different in math than it does in history.* You can make it more or less complex depending on the age of the students you teach. What my French teacher did for my classmate after he kept forgetting his work, do that up top for everyone. The kids who don't require the support will scoff, and some of us NDSOC might too as we might be in denial of this support need of ours, but you can also ask the more easily organized kids to share strategies they've developed that might help their classmates, which also avoids NDSOC feeling called out or ashamed that they need this to be demonstrated to them, and helps the other students feel essential instead of slowed down by having to support their peers.

Technology has obviously made organization much easier if tools are employed effectively, and therein lies the conundrum. I know the use or exclusion of technology is a hot-button issue and may be out of your control, but *if it's possible to use organization tools, not only should they be suggested, take the time to go over the interface of a few different ones with students, and follow up to see if they've chosen one and how it's going.* The first time I remember an educator not just lecturing us on organization but actually spending valuable class time on such programs was in (checks notes) 20th grade, and we only had 15 class periods per subject in my doctoral program, but half of an early one was about these tools, and it benefited me immensely as I worked my way through my studies.

A couple of chapters ago I recommended pairing/buddies to help with executive function. I want to add to that takeaway by bringing in what Ellie said helped support her with memory lapses. "I think that one thing that I really really latch on to for this topic is complementary cognition," she explained. "I had a friend who was very high anxious where I would leave my backpack on the bus and she would look before we got off the bus like, 'Is your backpack there?' And so I had like a lot of people I think that would just compensate for that for me." It might take time to suss out which kids have different cognitive styles, so this is more of an addendum to the previous pairing suggestion to say, *explain that students will eventually be paired up, and that the pairing will be based on supporting each other not just regarding deadlines but also memory and other characteristics.* I can hear you saying, "won't the neurodivergent child be embarrassed about clearly being told what they need, especially if they haven't been diagnosed?"

And, maybe. And some of us will reject the plan the way some people reject group work out of hand. But even if this aspect of the pairing is seen as highlighting a deficit, as you read on you'll see what some of our exceptional strengths are, and so we would be leading our classmates in different ways. If you stop here, and only suggest pairs that frame a possibly neurodivergent student of color as a burden, yes, it won't go well. But hopefully by the end of the book you'll see that there are things that only we can do and model for our peers, and we might not only be *seen* as valuable, but begin to *feel* that way about ourselves.

Notes

1 Cowan, N. (2008) What Are the Differences between Long-Term, Short-Term, and Working Memory? *Progress in Brain Research* 169, 323–338. https://doi.org/10.1016/S0079-6123(07)00020-9

2 https://www.thegoodtrade.com/features/doom-boxes/#:~:text=It's%20not%20just%20neurodivergent%20folks,stuff%20or%20too%20little%20space.

3 https://www.bigissue.com/opinion/neurodivergent-tax-is-a-price-autistic-people-like-me-have-to-pay/

4 Bangma, D.F., Koerts, J., Fuermaier, A.B.M., Mette, C., Zimmermann, M., Toussaint, A.K., Tucha, L., and Tucha, O. (2019) Financial Decision-Making in Adults with ADHD. *Neuropsychology* 33 (8), 1065–1077. https://doi.org/10.1037/neu0000571

6

Staying Out of View
On Masking and Its Psychological Toll

Back in the first chapter, I wrote about being seen as disruptive in the classroom and the way that affected some of us. But not all of the interviewees told me that was their reputation. In fact, plenty told me quite the opposite, that they did everything possible to stay out of view, and many of them said that a lot of that had to do with what was expected of them as girls.

As you may have noticed, everyone you've heard from so far, aside from me and my own stories, is a woman or was at least assigned female at birth – *I did interview one man, but his responses will factor in later.* This entire book is about an underexplored intersectional identity, but gender expectations add yet another wrinkle to the story. To be a female(-identified) student of color who is also an undiagnosed neurodivergent is to face a set of challenges I myself can't claim to have had to face.

Claire Sibonney of *The Washington Post* recently covered this issue and explained the results accordingly:

> A 2016 study[1] found that, by 10th grade, White children are nearly twice as likely to receive a diagnosis for ADHD than Black children. The study's lead author, Tumaini Rucker Coker, head of general pediatrics at Seattle

DOI: 10.4324/9781003465126-7

Children's Hospital and a top researcher at its Center for Child Health, Behavior and Development, said that while her study didn't look at underdiagnosis of Black girls, Education Department data shows telling signs of racial and gender discrimination in diagnosing ADHD: Black girls are six times more likely to be suspended from school than White girls.

Coker explained that behavior as common as talking back in class could have wildly different consequences, depending on how it is interpreted. For Black girls, it is often viewed as "intimidation" of a teacher.

There's that "intimidation" word again.

There are a few things in this excerpt worth calling attention to. First, the underdiagnosis statistics, which, like I said, I don't want to wallow in, are dire. Second, even for a scholar who is an expert on such things, like Dr. Coker, the research still doesn't yet focus on the subsections featured in this chapter. And third, the consequences are severe. As Sibonney wrote in that same article, "Researchers and therapists said they are especially worried about those undiagnosed or undertreated," adjectives that describe everyone I spoke to.

In Monique Morris's book *Pushout*,[2] she chronicles the way that Black girls in particular are presumed to be troublesome, and reframes the commonly accepted narrative that this population eagerly drops out into the reality that they are, as the title says, pushed out. Obviously not all girls of color are neurodivergent, but when you think about the challenges shared thus far in this book, and you consider what the additional consequences are if they step out of line, the reason that many of the people I interviewed tried so hard not to stand out is clear. But, as I've written already, it's pretty hard for us NDSOC not to make ourselves seen in one way or another.

Counter-Narratives

"I was the quiet kid," Rachel told me. "Painfully shy. Growing up, my dad, who's Mexican-American, I think the message was, 'you respect your teachers.' You're in school for a reason. You don't want to get in trouble. So I was very careful not to get in trouble. I took that message to heart. So I was very, very quiet, very, very shy."

In contrast to whatever loud nonsense I was doing, many of the people I spoke to were experiencing many of the same chaotic thought processes that I was, but were taking great pains to stifle all of their expression, or, horror of horrors, admit that they were in need of support.

"I was, what is it, twice exceptional or whatever," Rachel said. "So they put me in a gifted program or whatever. But that made it worse for me because then I was like, 'Well, I super better not, I really better not admit I don't know something.' So, you know, it started to become a problem when math concepts got harder. So I do struggle with math. Just like a lot of ADHD people do, dyscalculia. And yeah, I think just the big thing is I never wanted to admit that I didn't know."

For some of them, hiding was even more difficult.

"I think 'staying out of view' is probably pretty well said," Robyn said. "Not only being a Black kid and in a mostly white space. I was also [exceptionally] tall pretty, pretty early . . . I felt like I stood out a lot and that didn't feel super safe."

This wasn't just their perception, though. Sometimes they were told directly that speaking up was not going to be welcomed by either their peers or their teachers themselves. Marie told me that she sometimes felt like her moments of enthusiasm were seen as burdensome rather than beneficial much of the time:

I was always masking, like, I always had more than I wanted to say, or more than I wanted to do, but I couldn't do it in the confines of certain classrooms, because I learned that it wasn't safe to do that. Whether that meant speaking up or asking more questions or having a discussion and exploring a topic further. I was not always welcomed in doing that. And it was either because the classroom was full of students who didn't want to want that to happen like they viewed it as me creating more work for them. Like if I ask a question on the homework, and the teachers are like, 'Yeah, let's do blah, blah, blah,' then the students would get mad and they were like, 'Great, now we have more work to do.' Or the teachers were viewing it as me creating more work because they didn't want to dive into that discussion or go down that rabbit hole with me.

I want to talk about the use of "masking" in a second because it's a key to the neurodivergent experience, but first, note that Marie, just like Robyn, mentioned feeling unsafe in educational environments. If there's one thing we should absolutely feel in school, it's psychological and emotional safety, and one of the sub-themes that will continue to poke its way through the text of these interviews is just how unsafe the interviewees often felt, while also feeling unable to voice their fear. And this feeling, living in a state of fear, is traumatic, despite the fact that it doesn't really meet the traditional definition. I wrote about this elsewhere, and I call what happened to us "low-drama trauma" or what one of my therapists called "trauma with a little t." This is not to say that our lives may not have been more traditionally traumatic in other ways, as you've heard from a few of the speakers with difficult home lives, but these anecdotes carry real pain all the same, even if they wouldn't make a very compelling movie plot. I'm drilling down on this to underline the point that the strategies that I hope people develop based on these counternarratives are indeed a form of trauma-informed teaching, even if they're unlikely to ever be described as such – feeling fearful about asking for support is not going to be added to the official list of Adverse Childhood Experiences (ACEs) anytime soon. This is not really a criticism of trauma-informed teaching, but I do believe that, although there are resources on combining anti-racism and trauma-informed education as well as guidance on neurodivergence and trauma, there remains a lack of information bringing all three things together, and I hope that these stories can begin to shift the conversation to recognize these seemingly small but nonetheless impactful experiences we have had.

Back to masking then, and not the kind we should definitely have done more often than we did during the pandemic.

No, in this case "masking" refers to "the process of intentionally, or unintentionally, hiding aspects of yourself to avoid harm."[3] It's certainly not *exclusive* to neurodivergent people – you've probably done it at some point, especially if you're part of any sort of marginalized group – but for us, it's a habit we develop once we learn that our true selves are likely to be rejected. As the article cited above explains, masking over long periods of time causes great mental strain and can have serious mental health consequences – study participants also said it left them extremely fatigued and miserable. I am sure you can imagine how being tired and miserable could detract from a student's ability to learn, and then you can add the fact that, from an outside perspective, masking isn't really visible – which is the point of the "mask" after all – so it sure doesn't look like we're doing enough to warrant feeling out of energy, leaving us simultaneously depleted and, if we decide to share, risking being categorized as overly dramatic. But, especially for a child, when the potential alternative is being ostracized, it's not exactly a difficult decision, and it's not like we can predict we're going to suffer years in the future. Truth be told, it's not even always conscious, but can sometimes just be a natural means of trying to protect ourselves.

Masking is perhaps the experience that has bonded me the most to neurodivergent people I've spoken to, both for this project and otherwise. Every conversation I've had with a new ND friend, masking seems to come up, and the relative lightness we feel when we don't have to do it is a joy that's hard to describe unless you've experienced it yourself. The problem now is of course less school and more about work and other sorts of interpersonal relationships, but that's not to say it doesn't have anything to do with our K-12 experiences. Indeed, the way our ability (or lack thereof) to relate to our peers and teachers shaped our approach to interaction has long-lasting ripple effects. Besides, when seeking an adult evaluation for yourself, the three contexts in which your neurodivergence needs to impact your life in order for you to qualify are not just school but also work and relationships.

Problems in school are hard enough, but it's often possible to muddle your way through. As an adult, though, struggling with relationships could lead to a divorce or other types of family strife; struggling with work can ruin your career. And wouldn't you know it, although statistics are too varied to be useful – especially given unreliable rates of diagnosis – all available evidence suggests that we tend to have a hard time maintaining strong marriages, especially when married to someone who isn't also ND.[4] Similarly, our careers are often spotty and peripatetic,[5] which increases financial instability and also makes it harder to seek and afford treatment. Additionally, the qualitative and quantitative data cited is about all races of neurodivergent people, which implies that the statistics would be even worse for neurodivergent people of color, although I can't technically assert that for sure because, as ever, we're underdiagnosed and thus rarely qualify for official studies, and they rarely think to ask about us anyway.

It was ultimately masking that finally got me to seek evaluation and neurodivergence-specific treatment. In the early fall of 2021, my then-employer told us we'd need to return to the in-person office, and I started freaking out. It wasn't so much for safety concerns – I had my shots and, annoying as it would have been, I didn't really mind putting a (physical) mask on a couple of days a week – and so I was really surprised by how stressed out the prospect of the office made me. This was the same job where my supervisor had been upset with what I now know were neurodivergent traits, but she'd been upset about that even when we were fully remote, and I almost lost my job entirely in 2020 because I kept making small editing errors when I couldn't lie to myself that we were being given more than what was quite obviously busywork. And besides, through sheer spite I'd managed to somewhat repair my reputation with leadership in the year since my career had been imperiled. No, it was something else, and I couldn't put my finger on it.

This came a year and a half after I'd started considering the possibility that I might be neurodivergent through a combination of professional treatment for mood disorders and, by chance, taking a doctoral class on disability research and justice with the woman who had since become my dissertation advisor and a – maybe *the* – central figure in my development as a scholar – *Hi, Dr. V!* I had submitted a proposal to write an academic chapter in a book about disability policy and experience, and I'd used that same "definition of irk" anecdote to see if my story would be worth telling. It was accepted, and so I'd spent the intervening time trying to dig into this whole new aspect of myself, even though I'd never been assessed in any way. I figured I'd go for an evaluation after my son was born, but he was born in February of 2020 so I think you know why those plans changed.

Anyway, so now it was late 2021, and I did more research to see if it was possible that the ADHD I suspected I had could have been a reason for my office anxiety, and the more I looked into it, the more I realized that, despite how monumentally stressful the past year and a half had been for many reasons between the lockdown, the overall news, raising an infant and then a toddler with my wife, and almost losing my job, *all while still being a student*, I was nonetheless a lot more relaxed than I had been in the years beforehand. And I realized that for me, being in the office with my coworkers was such a daily grind that I felt more at ease going through All Of That than sitting at a desk near them all week long.

Now, there are some sensory reasons that factored into this – we had an "open" office that meant I could hear every bit of background noise, and people walked by my desk all day, which was incredibly distracting – but we'll talk about those in a later chapter on that topic. Ultimately, though, what I realized is that I had never felt comfortable being myself around my coworkers, who were from very different walks of life than I was, were mostly somewhat older, and, sadly, not averse to making jokes and comments about disability and mental health. There were two or three I got along with, and another two I made general small talk with about the Yankees, but I spent all day shrinking inside of myself, except when I got a chance to actually teach, which was unfortunately rare. My evaluation helped me connect this feeling to how I'd tried to protect myself in the classroom, and revealed that my mostly detached and distant demeanor in the workplace was essentially an emotional callus that was easier to employ than my years spent trying to forge connections and just feeling excluded nonetheless. I also realized that every time I've struggled at work it's been tied to either a neurodivergent trait more generally, masking in particular, or the emotional outbursts that can result when you just can't mask anymore. (*See Chapter 10 for more on emotional volatility.*)

You see, once we've grown accustomed to masking, we tend to employ this in every situation where we're surrounded by people we're uncertain will welcome the full version of ourselves we're most comfortable with, but despite its short-term convenience, masking is ultimately unhealthy and takes a tremendous toll, and an unhealthy person placed under strain in a relationship, a job, or both is certainly likely not to perform to the very best of their abilities. It's not a K-12 teacher's responsibility to fix the prospects of a neurodivergent worker or spouse, but if we can develop healthier patterns during childhood and adolescence, we stand a much better chance of emerging into adulthood on sturdier ground, and without the need to try and protect ourselves by hiding who we really are.

A big part of why our experiences are distinct from those of white neurodivergent students is the range of emotions and behaviors we are "allowed" to display. There are certainly limitations on what I could show as a Black boy, and those are damaging, but, as the interviewees told me, being quiet as a girl of color is not something that will strike a teacher as abnormal, so it was a relatively easy mask to slip on.

Despite harmful media discourse, parents of color do an excellent job overall at supporting their – or, our – children's racial identities, far beyond the messages they receive in their classrooms. Scholars refer to this process as "ethnic-racial socialization",[6] and it serves a vital protective function for our children as they navigate a world that can be extremely hostile to them, both outside of and inside the school building. Students who are accurately diagnosed with conditions that fall under the neurodivergent umbrella can receive official treatment and support along these lines as well, but given the oft-cited disparity in diagnosis rates, no matter how good a job we might do with supporting our children's racial identity, they are rarely equipped to deal with these aspects of their humanity. When I say "equipped" I mean only in the sense of not being provided the necessary tools, as a healthy neurodivergent life does require expertise; I have no doubt our parents are capable of the love we need, as mine certainly always demonstrated theirs. But if you don't know what you don't know, you can't really do much about it, and both children and parents alike will remain confused and distressed as the child moves through school behind a mask that feels like a comfortable refuge.

"When I was a kid," Rose said, "my solution was just talk less. And I could get away with that more easily. Typically as a girl it's the whole idea of girls are to be seen not heard kind of thing. It wasn't a concern to most people that I would just not talk . . . Thinking about whether it was conscious or unconscious, it's like, in some ways, it's conscious.

"How do I avoid negative outcomes, which is probably not like the exact words I was thinking when I was a child, but that's really just what it is," she continued. "And I think imitating the behavior patterns or speech patterns of other people. I think that I copied my sister a lot, because she was a lot more outgoing than me, which she would get annoyed about. We were constantly always bickering and I don't know. I probably wouldn't have admitted it as much at the time, but I think that the reason that I was doing a lot of that is because being me wasn't really working."

It's tough to hold it together when you feel like being you isn't working. You'll note that most of the stories I share here are from sixth grade and later. It's not because I don't remember anything before that, it's because I didn't really start masking until fourth or fifth grade, and, whatever may have happened before that, it all felt ten times worse when I was trying to be someone other than myself.

Despite the moments you've heard about in this book, I was an extremely silly little boy who loved going on adventures in the park and making up superheroes like Fireman (*you see, he was actually made of fire. I was very creative*) and Dangerous (*look, I was really into that 1991 Michael Jackson album. So many bygone problematic faves*). Even after I skipped a grade, I knew I didn't quite fit in with the older kids, but I didn't really change until we started having to follow a schedule and travel around the school building by ourselves. Once the need to organize and perform academically came into the picture, I felt more and more stress, and so, the times I was teased for having interests that were deemed too childish hurt more than it had in the past, and over several years I slowly tried to stuff the little kid I was into a box and forget about him. I made jokes in class, yes, but I was imitating the kids around me, and since I didn't actually understand their behavior patterns, like Rose said above, the humor didn't land and nothing seemed to work, all of which eventually led to the emotional calluses that had distanced me from my colleagues at my previous job.

"You know, I definitely put a lot of effort into kind of being in the, in the shadows without being too much in the shadows," Whitney told me. "It's like the kids that are too in the shadows, the teachers do notice them because they're kind of going way off in the deep end.

"I didn't have a lot of friends," she added. "I had like a friend or two that I would, you know, actually talk to and like I think that kind of helped me stay in the shadows in a lot of ways because it wasn't like I was a loner, but I also wasn't flush with friends. And, you know, I think because I was turning in my assignments and I wasn't disruptive. I was following the rules. And I think for me, I thought, 'well, if I just follow the rules and don't raise any awareness, I can stay in the shadows,' even though I was maybe struggling with some of the content."

As she said, especially for girls, if you're not making a lot of noise and you're not actually failing your assignments, then the stress that's occurring behind the mask can be very easy to miss if you don't know what to look for.

As for me, I eventually got a new job, and during that interview process I decided to take the risk and be open about how I was, because I knew if I was hired and had to hide myself again, I'd run into the same issues I've had in all my previous jobs, and I was determined to see what it was like to be comfortable in my own skin while doing my work. Wouldn't you know, I've never performed better at a job than I have at this one, but I got very very lucky to find an inclusive workplace that not only tolerates my methods but embraces me and my exceptions, and that's not something all of us can say. Many of the other NDSOC I've met still have to stuff their whole selves into a small and stifling box just to get through the day. Having to mask makes it much harder to be successful, much harder to be "productive," and much harder to find the joy we deserve.

Takeaways

There's only really one main takeaway here: *make your classroom a place where students feel comfortable lowering their masks.* It's easy enough for me when I teach, because I tell my students about my neurodivergence, partially so they won't be unnerved when I don't look them in the eye, but I do think this helps people open up and feel supported in doing so. If you yourself are not neurodivergent, you can still metaphorically lower your mask, whether that means opening up about strategically chosen aspects of your identity – *whatever you feel is safe for you to do professionally, of course* – or struggles you yourself have had with organization or memory or what have you. Younger students might not even really know how much work they're doing to try and blend in, and displaying your own unconventionality in some way might give them the strength to lean into what makes them who they are. As Whitney said, NDSOC may be just "riding in the middle," even if stereotypes of rambunctious white male students suggest we would always be calling attention to ourselves and our neurodivergent traits, so hearing this from our teachers might help us find the safety we need. Rose also suggests explicitly highlighting the talents of students who may not feel confident in displaying traditionally outgoing behavior.

Ultimately, masking is one of the hardest parts of neurodivergence, and one of the hardest habits to break. It's even harder for NDSOC, and harder still for minoritized genders within that group. Whatever you can do to help us feel like it's okay to really show our faces will make it so we don't have to spend decades hidden, even long after we're out of your classroom.

Notes

1   https://publications.aap.org/pediatrics/article-abstract/138/3/e20160407/77132/Racial-and-Ethnic-Disparities-in-ADHD-Diagnosis?redirectedFrom=fulltext

2   Morris, M. (2016) *Pushout: The Criminalization of Black Girls in Schools*. New York: The New Press.

3   Miller, D., Rees, J., and Pearson, A. (2021) "Masking Is Life": Experiences of Masking in Autistic and Nonautistic Adults. *Autism Adulthood* 3 (4), 330–338. doi:10.1089/aut.2020.0083. Epub 2021 Dec 7. PMID: 36601640; PMCID: PMC8992921.

4   See https://www.additudemag.com/adhd-marriage-statistics-personal-stories/ for more narratives.

5   Davies, J., Heasman, B., Livesey, A., Walker, A., Pellicano, E., and Remington, A. (2023) Access to Employment: A Comparison of Autistic, Neurodivergent and Neurotypical Adults' Experiences of Hiring Processes in the United Kingdom. *Autism: The International Journal of Research and Practice* 27 (6), 1746–1763. https://doi.org/10.1177/13623613221145377

6   Burnett M, McBride M, Green MN, Cooper SM. (2022) "When I Think of Black Girls, I Think of Opportunities": Black Girls' Identity Development and the Protective Role of Parental Socialization in Educational Settings. *Frontiers in Psychology* Jul 25; 13:933476. doi:10.3389/fpsyg.2022.933476. PMID: 35959072; PMCID: PMC9358241.

7

Following Recipes
On the Trouble with Multi-Step Instructions

Have you ever put something together from IKEA? I'm sure you have. They send it to you and it's in pieces, right? So it's your job to follow the directions to turn your pile of slabs into a bookcase or a shelf or whatever. People swear to me that they love IKEA instructions, but it's the most frustrating thing on the planet to me because I never know what the pictures actually mean. You usually get a little blob of a man in pictures using various tools to construct your piece of furniture, but for me, my brain turns all of the images around and makes it impossible for me to just do what the images suggest. I once spent literally nine hours putting together a dresser because halfway through I realized I'd been doing part of it entirely upside down, but admitting that I didn't really understand was too high a hurdle to even attempt, and that was in my 30s.

Around the same time, I spent the entire first semester of my doctoral program citing only open-access scholarship because the instructions given to me by my school for making use of the school's journal access were too lengthy, and I just happened to get lucky that what I wanted was posted online for anyone to read and download. The fact of the matter is that, after a certain

DOI: 10.4324/9781003465126-8

number of steps, folks like me are going to lose focus and try to get things done as efficiently as possible, and that can lead to a lot of trouble, especially in an education system where your assessment is sometimes based on how well you follow instructions. And yes, this chapter is very closely related to the "coloring outside the lines" discussion from earlier, but in this case we are specifically talking about multi-step instructions given to us and on which we are assessed.

But truly, why does it matter if we follow multi-step instructions to the letter? It's been said that life will require following a series of steps so it's important that schools prepare us for this, but ultimately this is just inducting us into a tradition of harm. Tema Okun's influential essay on White Supremacy Culture[1] discusses the danger of adherence to the One Right Way ideology, and I think what we've seen thus far will back up what was written:

One right way shows up as:

- the belief there is one right way to do things and once people are introduced to the right way, they will see the light and adopt it;
- when a person or group does not adapt or change to "fit" the one right way, then those defining or upholding the one right way assume something is wrong with the other, those not changing, not with us;
- similar to a missionary who sees only value in their beliefs about what is good rather than acknowledging value in the culture of the communities they are determined to "convert" to the right way of thinking and/or the right way of living.[2]

I know it might seem, from what everyone in this book has said, that we'd embrace a long, detailed list of steps for completing a task, but for many of us, there's a limit to how many we're willing to follow if we can possibly see a faster way, and therein lies the conflict that causes us so much tension in both school and life.

Counter-Narratives

"It's infuriating to me when something is not efficient," Robyn told me. And I want to be clear that despite how it might seem from the outside, we are not inclined to take shortcuts to be lazy or to avoid doing due diligence, we just abhor what feels to us like wasting time. When given a long list of steps, Robyn said, "I'm doing all those steps. I'm doing all the steps and I will be very . . . I don't want it to be 20 steps. I want it to be the least number of steps that it needs to be to make sense. Like I will be irritated at the lack of efficiency, but I will do all the steps."

It's one thing to be somewhat exasperated by having to follow instructions we deem to be inefficient, but sometimes these directions are actually confusing, and then we return to the same issue of needing to ask questions to fill in the gaps that more neurotypical educators might assume we understand. Rose explained her thought process in seeking additional information that's not always contained in assignments:

> I might just pretend like I understand to get out of the situation. So I sometimes ended up like, in a weird, stressful interaction, particularly as a kid. I think now, as an adult, I feel more comfortable asking people to repeat themselves. Asking questions to clarify because somebody might give you 10 steps versus specific instructions, but there's actually a whole bunch of information missing. And so I have no problem asking questions. I know that there's eventually a point where you start to irritate people because of too many questions but people are not aware of how unclear they're being. And I know that some of it is me in my interpretation, but I think it's been really important to get more comfortable using asking questions as a tool. I think that admitting that I have difficulties with processing auditory information or verbal instructions. I've experimented with doing that, but I think that people don't know what to do with that information. People think that means you're hearing impaired, which is not the same thing . . . Unless I've known somebody

for a long time, telling them that is not helpful to me. It creates more problems because then they're like, 'Okay, are you mentally challenged?' That's kind of like 'okay, let me not try that, let me not say it that way,' or get to know this person better and then like, basically if I tell somebody this before they decide I'm capable, then I'm just undercutting myself is kind of how it feels.

Most teachers work extremely hard at making their instructions comprehensible to their students, and most of us understand that assignments we're given have been pored over for clarity. Consequently, asking for additional guidance can feel like admitting to a lack of intelligence, or at the very least painting ourselves as absent-minded, when, no matter how hard we try and concentrate, we might just skip a step or five if our brain decides that's the best way to get something done.

This chapter is called "following recipes" because those are examples of multi-step instructions where it's usually quite important to follow the directions to the letter, at least if you want a good meal anyway. Most of us aren't responsible for cooking while we're K-12 students, but the impression we received from our teachers was that assignments were indeed like baking a cake, and that if we didn't do them exactly as prescribed, we'd end up with a finished product that deserved to be thrown into the trash. There's a logic to this adherence to following instructions, to some extent; even job applications will "test" applicants by steering them towards certain avenues of interaction and dismiss people who don't do what's asked of them. Think of the job ads that say "no calls" – if you do call, you'll be rejected for refusing to do what was asked of you, even if you might otherwise be qualified. Some of you reading this might argue that it's a part of your responsibilities as an educator to prepare your students for the reality of a world where instructions are often vital, but on the other hand, for us NDSOC, it really doesn't matter how important we're told that the recipe's steps are: we're just going to do it in the order that makes the most sense to us, even if the cake doesn't end up rising. It's a challenge, of course, because you clearly don't have the time to write out several different sets of instructions for each neurotype you might have in your classroom, so the question becomes how best to make a central set of instructions crystal clear to people who think the way that we do.

Whitney laughed when I asked her about following multi-step instructions, then related her school experiences to the relationship she currently has with her wife:

> I'm laughing because, it's unrelated, but it *is* related. My partner always laughs at me because cooking, there'll be instructions on the back of a box and like how to do it, and I will literally do it wrong. I will do step one, three, and four, and I will skip the other steps and she's like, 'you literally skipped step two.' And I'm like, 'No, I didn't. I read the whole thing. I did it.' Anyways, the answer is yes, I have a hard time following long lists of instructions. In the middle things just start to get blurry. And I'm like, 'I think I remember what that said.' And so I just like create the A-to-B bridge in my head. And it's not the right A-to-B bridge often. And I think in schools specifically, I think because of how I was, I really spent a lot of time making sure I wasn't bringing that extra attention to myself. So I would spend extra on my homework when I would get home. I wasn't rushing through my homework. I was sitting there for a couple hours working on it. So I had to make sure I did it right. And maybe like subconsciously segmenting the instructions where I could. I'm thinking more about school, but ultimately the answer is yes, I've always struggled with following long lists of instructions. How have I gotten through like that in academic situations? Some of that is a good question. I mean, truthfully, there were classes like accounting for example, and statistics where I really struggled because there were so many steps in like, calculating things. Like I failed that class. I had to retake that class because I just like I couldn't process how to do it right and they weren't good at explaining it.

Her story here captures a few of the things I would like to convey in this chapter, namely how it feels for us and how hard it can be for us to overcome without support. When she says that she will be utterly convinced that she's followed every step to the letter despite having skipped two or three, that's what makes it all so difficult. Once there's a certain amount of information to try and process, our brains just filter out what they think we don't need to care about, and it feels a little bit like blacking out for a period of time so short you don't even notice, nor can you successfully anticipate it. You will be staring directly at a list, and your eyes will just skip over a part of it, even if you swear you've double- and triple-checked. And it's embarrassing to get to the end of a task or an assignment and realize you just didn't do an important part of the process, not because you didn't care, but because your brain went into fast-forward at an inopportune time. As Whitney said, "things just start to get blurry," and then you come out on the other side dumbfounded about why you screwed up, and because you can't articulate what happened or why, you just come off as sloppy or lackadaisical, which is not the reputation you want to have in the classroom. Additionally, as Whitney said towards the end, sometimes, no matter how hard we try to follow the instructions we've been given, we never completely figure it out, and that can result in serious damage to our academic progress. Plenty of educators struggle to provide instructions in a way that will work best for our neurotypes, but on the other hand, especially pre-diagnosis, even we may not be able to articulate exactly what we need, so that just leaves us trying our very best to stay afloat and sometimes sinking anyway.

I also want to note her comments about her brain supplying "the A-to-B bridge" even if she'd missed a step. This is one of the things people need to understand about us, and why the advice to "just slow down" doesn't always work. We are going to fill in the gaps automatically, and we just might fill them in incorrectly, leading us down a path away from the actual goals of the assignment. We can spend extra time like Whitney did, and catch some of our errors, but the fast-forward button is going to activate and lead us astray when our assessment is tied to rigid expectations. It's a scary feeling to know there's always a chance you've missed something important, and, in reading this, I hope the message comes across that this tension increases the more steps we're given at a time.

Now, it's much easier for us to describe what we'd need from instructions, or even exactly how many steps is too many for us to handle. "It totally depends on how dense each step is," Marie said. "But I would say about eight. Number eight, I'm like, I don't know, I gotta gotta back out, or I gotta figure out a way to consolidate these instructions into less depth. You know, because that's just too many. I mean, maybe 10 is too much, but I would say if I'm being realistic, I tap out around eight.

"If it has to be exactly 300 grams of blah, blah substance," she continued, "I was thinking like, thank God I had a lab partner because otherwise I would have probably just glossed over some of that. You know, and then you have a lab partner who's like, 'no, no, we need to do this correctly.' I'm like, okay, good. I will as long as you helped me do it. You know, I had, I mean, almost in that sense, someone sort of body doubling with me, which helps a lot. But if it was just up to me, I probably would have cut corners where I could."

Her statement here recalls Ellie's earlier recommendation for complementary cognition, but, even though I've already suggested pairs and buddies, sometimes that's just not going to be feasible on, say, a purely individual assignment, and given the shame we often feel about our inability to avoid these pitfalls, we may well not openly share the fact that we've skipped a step and just sit there hoping we don't get found out.

"When there's so many steps," Rachel explained. "I will always forget something. And it's not even about forgetting, I swear that I can read all the instructions, and a certain thing will not compute and it'll be missing. And so I got really good at doing things on the fly when it comes to like adding, like maybe it said, 'make sure to include X, Y, and Z' and I only did X and Y. The day of, I'd be really good at adding Z because I would realize that my friends said that they had that part of it or I'd see it on another project. So I would often have to work on the fly in that way. But I swear if there were instructions, detailed instructions, there would always be something missing from my project. And it's not negligence . . . But with ADHD brain, some things just don't compute at certain times."

I want to be clear that I didn't ask anyone about negligence – all of us had experienced being assumed not to care. It followed me all the way up through my career. A colleague rolled out a new process that we were all expected to follow, and the instructions were several pages long, and I, like Marie said, tapped out. When I mentioned this to my colleague, she told me to try harder. I bring up this story about work because when she said that, it just brought me back to the way I'd frequently felt as a child.

I remember being punished once in a very archaic way and being asked to write out "I will not lie" like I was Bart Simpson in the opening credits. After a few pages of this, I realized I could save a little time and write "I won't lie," but when I tried to explain this, I was accused of laziness. It was around that time that I realized that for many authority figures, quantity mattered more than anything else. Perhaps out of spite, my approach towards my work gradually changed once I came to this new understanding. I still liked some of my classes, but instead of struggling through the others, when I found an assignment less than compelling but still wanted to be assessed positively, I started following the most basic of instructions obsessively, to an almost comical level. Paper was supposed to be six pages? I will give you exactly six pages. 5,000 words? Not one word more or less. Need to cite at least 10 sources? I'll give you one guess how many I'd use. Since I had accepted that I would always get something wrong or that my brain would go on fast-forward when it shouldn't, I figured the one thing I could always control was basic structural requirements such as these. It turned into something of a game for me, and I was far more interested in these little goals than the material I was supposed to be learning, yet I did get the assignments done. The sad thing is, this really did improve my standing among my teachers, and the message I received was that all that mattered was doing enough to make sure I was checking off boxes on a rubric. It took me several years to regain joy in writing, and in fact I was well into my 30s by that point. Perhaps subconsciously I kept going to school because I wanted to love writing again the way I had when I was a small child. Ultimately, it's the difference between output and (learning) outcomes, and I assure you that the years I spent focused primarily on output were not years in which I was learning nearly as much as I should have been. Several of these interviewees concurred with me when I recalled how this led to my acing standardized tests, not so much by becoming an expert at, say, reading comprehension itself but by looking at the questions and searching for the specific words in the text. This is a great way to outsmart the system but not a great way to increase your knowledge, but that's the message we got and so it's what we did. And since doing poorly on standardized tests is how many of our white peers were identified, this also extended the time it took for us to receive the support we needed.

Takeaways

In my work as a curriculum developer, I always keep myself and my fellow neurodivergent folks in mind when I'm writing out instructions, and there are some, at my previous job, who have thought I don't provide enough steps to ensure I cover all the bases. I understand the impulse to give out as much information as possible, but I also know that someone reading it might think the way I do, and I don't want to increase the cognitive load when it's not absolutely necessary. The way I prefer to write out instructions is to be very clear as to what steps need to be followed to the letter, which are important but contain wiggle room, and which are up to the students' (or participants') discretion. And this checkbox-rubric assessment doesn't end at K-12, of course; when I first was taught how to write a Literature Review in (checks notes again) 19th grade, it was largely graded on containing specific elements. But not entirely though, because an extremely impactful bit of guidance that that professor gave me was to demonstrate my voice in my writing, even if I still needed to hit certain explicit benchmarks. This was key for me, and is the central aspect of the takeaways for this chapter, because there will always be some boxes you have to tick, some steps you just can't skip, both in life and to receive good grades. Finding that balance between rigidity and freedom is a common theme for supporting folks like us, and multi-step instructions are a pertinent example of how that comes into play.

And so, the simplest takeaway is to *only write down the steps that are absolutely necessary to complete a particular assignment*. Not everything you'd do or even everything you'd recommend we do in completing a task needs to be included as part of the body of a set of instructions – I would boil it down to the barest set of steps and then include possible options as sidebars, footnotes, links, or what have you. Additionally, in writing out said instructions, *write with fluidity and humanity wherever possible as a way of drawing us in*. The warmth will help us view the assignment as more collaborative than antagonistic and is less likely to lead to us just giving you the pages or words requested without any emotional investment.

Rose suggested that requests for verbal instructions to be repeated should be not only accepted but encouraged, the same way you'd absolutely do the same for a student who had trouble hearing and had an official accommodation. In fact, a lot of the suggestions in this book are essentially Unofficial Accommodations since we're unlikely to be diagnosed, so if you'd do it when mandated, expect there's a child in front of you who might benefit from the same adjustments anyway.

I do tend to think that this chapter certainly applies more to older students, as not only are classes and assignments more complex but written instructions naturally require reading. Teachers of young children, I have to believe, fully understand you can only give out so many instructions at a time without overwhelming your students. For reasons that I can't quite explain, even though it's not surprising, as school becomes more "academic," this warmth and patience is less emphasized, something I certainly experienced with my more upsetting experiences having occurred from sixth grade onward. Now, if you're thinking that I'm implying a high school teacher should treat their sophomores and juniors like first graders, in some ways I am actually saying . . . yes, because, although not every elementary educator is a paragon of warmth, it's the loss of that emotional support that can leave us floundering, and there needs to be a shift towards grace and compassion for older children and adolescents, especially for us neurodivergent students of color.

Notes

1   See https://www.whitesupremacyculture.info/ for more information.
2   https://www.whitesupremacyculture.info/one-right-way.html

8

Turning the Volume Down

On Sensory Overload and Its Many Manifestations

The tricky thing about the topic of this chapter – sensory sensitivity and overload – is that it affects all of us differently. Not just in terms of the extent of sensitivity we might have, but also in that different major senses may or may not be issues for us, so solving for the issue is going to require a lot of trial-and-error. For the people in this book, we had to conduct that trial-and-error process ourselves, in some cases before we had the language to even explain what was bothering us. Other times, particular aspects of our physical discomfort were so constant and started early enough that we'd grown to accept that we may never be rid of a feeling that drove us up the wall. For some of us, it was visual distraction; for some of us, sound; for some of us, touch; I am certain smell and taste were impacted too, but those don't come up nearly as often in the classroom. The search for peace and comfort had the potential to completely derail our ability to learn, but because what got under our skin – sometimes literally – often felt relatively small, as you'll hear, it rarely made sense to ask for support. And truthfully, there is always some sort of sensory experience happening in a classroom, and if you had the power to completely control the volume of a group of students,

DOI: 10.4324/9781003465126-9

you would be a wizard, so, as ever, it's about finding a balance or helping us find our own balance so that we can be in the best position possible to learn.

I should add that sensory sensitivity is, I would wager, well-known enough for those with any familiarity with autism. What I didn't know until I started to piece my own neurology together was that this is true for all sorts of ND folks. And this isn't just a matter pertaining to doing well in school. Dr. Ludmila Praslova put in this way in an essay she penned about the need for sensory safety as a means of being inclusive towards the neurodivergent:

> Beeping sounds from equipment with low batteries. Coworkers on their phones. Flickering lights. Clashing colors. Smells of burnt food mixed with cleaning products. All of these are examples of sensory input that can become overwhelming and overstimulating. When sensory input exceeds our ability to process and cope with it, our mental and physical health suffers. In the workplace, performance suffers as well. In some cases, the lack of sensory safety can exclude highly qualified people from working.[1]

The sensory sensitivities we might have include, but are absolutely not limited to:

- ◆ Hyperacusis, or sensitivity to loud sounds.
- ◆ Misophonia, or sensitivity to *specific* sounds, which may or may not be loud. A common example is being unable to tolerate chewing.
- ◆ Sensitivity to certain types of light (e.g. fluorescent) or brightness in general.
- ◆ Various sensitivities to specific textures.

These traits are not limited to autism, or ADHD, or any particular type of neurodivergence, and when these sensitivities are triggered, it can lead to intense anxiety and anger, among other seemingly extreme reactions.[2] We'll talk more about the emotionality of it all in Chapter 10, but for now, all of us will share with you how this showed up for us in the classroom and otherwise.

Counter-Narratives

When I finally did go and get diagnosed, I was still of course working that job where I'd had some serious clashes with leadership over what turned out to be issues caused directly by neurodivergent traits. As I mentioned a few chapters ago, I was panicked about my office return for (neurodivergent) masking reasons, but I also did say that there were some sensory reasons I was so stressed out, all of which helped me understand why I spent so much of my classroom time unable to learn effectively, or at least not in the ways my institutions were pleased with, regardless of how well I always tested. At this job, I was originally seated near the door just by chance, and not only did that mean people always walked by right around my eye-line, but also, this being a government building the public couldn't just enter, when people forgot their security badges, I was the one who would have to stand up and let them in. This happened dozens of times a day it seemed, because people always seemed to forget their badge whenever they went out to the bathroom or to lunch.

I also realized that a big part of my panic was that I'd never been able to block out my coworkers' conversations, in particular when they tried to be polite and whisper. There was always something about the sound of whispering that set me on edge and made it impossible for me to focus. And also, the office was cold. Far from not being good at my actual job, I was, it turns out, constantly seeking refuge from stressors I'd always had, and the steps I've taken since then have made my life immeasurably calmer and more comfortable. I know what sort of visual environment I need to avoid being distracted involuntarily while also not preferring a blank wall where my mind will wander from the dullness. I either wear noise-canceling headphones or earplugs that merely lower the volume if I need to be in conversations, and I even changed my wardrobe so I almost never have to tuck in my shirt, because that was always a maddening feeling. But, again, I have a good, inclusive job, and enough time and money to really think through my needs. As a kid in a classroom? It was just sensory chaos for me and for everyone I spoke to.

"Big lights," Whitney said when I asked her about her sensory sensitivities. "I don't know if that relates to you, but like big lights, all the big lights being on? No, I can't function and I need the lights turned down . . . Even large crowds of people like I said earlier, like I didn't even have a lot of friends. I had one friend through grade school, one friend through middle school, one friend through high school that I really like, stuck around with. I'm trying to like think back, like what was like sensory overload. I mean, a lot of it again is like crowds, lights, a lot of sounds all happening at once."

As you might have already noticed and will continue to take note of, "crowds" and "big lights" are things that schools are chock full of, so I inquired what she did to deal with these issues in the time before she had more substantial support.

"I wish I could really tell you what I was doing," she replied. "I do think some of it I just suffered through and like, that is like the unfortunate part is like I think that there were clear signs but that I just kind of put my head down, grit my teeth and just suffered through a lot of those things. Because again, I also just didn't want to cause attention to my home life and what was going on. Even if that meant I was the one that had to suffer through like I did."

To repeat for what must be the millionth time by this point, these are the stories of the survivors, the ones who lived to tell the tales of being neurodivergent students of color, and even we have no real clue as to how we managed to stay afloat. Whitney does point out that, as much as she and many of the others in this book were suffering behind a mask, there were signs that I hope this book will make it easier for readers to pick up on. We might have been exceptional kids, but we were still kids, and all the tricks we pulled still didn't mean adults shouldn't have been able to pick up on the fact that we were hiding our struggles, but if programs aren't given the material with which to train their educators, the fact that a student like Whitney, whose brilliance I can vouch for, is under sensory siege at all times yet still pulls through is both a testament to her own ability and an indictment of her environments.

These weren't completely hidden signals, to be clear. "I remember I would leave the classroom a lot," she said. "I would just go on a Hall Pass or I would leave the classroom a lot and just go to the bathroom, but I wasn't going to the bathroom. I was just going to like, regulate again, and then I'd come back and continue doing what we were doing. In some ways that was me trying to cope like realizing I was overwhelmed and I would just leave the situation and come back." But then, if my own experience of not showing up to school for several days is any indication, it's possible to disappear without garnering attention, so long as you're doing well on the tests when the time comes.

Rachel told me about her auditory processing issues. "If things were too loud, and some teachers weren't, you know, able to get the class [under control]," she said, "if anyone was talking around me it would be very hard for me to pay attention to what the teacher was saying. Even if it was whispers, they are very distracting. And all those fricatives everywhere. Um, so yeah, audio is definitely where I had the sensory overload." (*Rachel is a language scholar, but for everyone else, fricatives are a group of sounds which are particularly hard to stifle, and if you're whispering, and most other sounds are quiet, they stand out even more. Examples include: [s], as in "sip," [z] as in "zip," [ʃ] as in "ship."*)

In the present day, long since out of the classroom, she still has to contend with these issues. "The same thing happens to me in movie theaters these days," she explained. "You know, if someone whispers I'm like, 'oh my god, that was the loudest thing I've ever heard.' It just becomes much more loud to me than if you were [speaking] louder."

Robyn said she basically malfunctions when she's distracted by certain sounds. "If there is talking going on," she said, "It's almost impossible for me to tune it out. My brain will focus on that to an unnecessary extent and it's too, too much. It's too much at the same time . . . I just can't I can't focus. Like I can't. I can't read. I can't focus on what I'm trying to do if that's happening. I probably short circuit." Like most of us, she's since developed compensation mechanisms so she can meet her professional obligations. "Now, I mean, if I'm working in the office, I have to have headphones in when I'm in a meeting and when I'm not in a meeting, I'll play music to drown out the noise of other people talking."

Marie told me about a common school building noise that many of you will recall, especially if you're older than a certain age, and a list of other sensory sensitivities that she experienced:

> I think auditory things were definitely a sensory night-mare for me. I hated in gym class as a kid, the big round fans that they had that were *so loud*. Oh, I hated those and they were always on and the teacher's trying to give you instructions, or tell you what the activity is for the day. And I was like, dying because I could not stop fix-ating on the noise of this loud fan. You know, I couldn't understand what my classmate was saying. So I think noise levels are very something I was super-sensitive to. I think sometimes lighting would be a problem like if we were trying to watch a movie in class and they had all the lights on. Like how am I supposed to focus on the screen? You know when you have every single light in this room on and so sometimes, like lighting was a little bit of an issue, but not as bad as the auditory issues that I had. And I mean, as an adult, I have these amazing soundproof headphones. And when I got them, I could feel my entire body relax, and I wish I had had these headphones in school as a kid. And if I could have had my headphones and listen to music or something when I was working, that would have changed the game for me, like I would have been so much more productive in my classroom, as opposed to having to take all my work home and work on it in an environment that I control. Like that would have made a huge difference because I wouldn't have had to struggle against the environment around me so much.

It was more than just distracting for her – she also told me about a time she'd become unsettled by a classmate's clicking pen during an exam and had been reprimanded for speaking when she asked her to stop. I need not remind everyone how we're more heavily and frequently punished than students who don't look like us, so we learn to keep these sensitivities to ourselves as much as possible and struggle through the discomfort unless and until we absolutely can't anymore.

When asked the same questions, Rose responded, "I would say, sound, light, people, extension of people as like social interactions, sounds of people, but also, I think, a lot of emotional stimuli. Like I tend to pick up on other people's emotions. I can't stop myself hearing everything that's going on around me to make it really hard to be in a restaurant because it's like a lot of challenges with signal to noise ratio. I can hear everybody's conversations at the same time, and it becomes very overstimulating, exhausting, and stressful.

"I think none of my teachers ever really noticed anything that was going on with me," she added, "internally or externally for the most part, unless I got in trouble. Like, there's always been a huge disconnect between what's going on in my internal world and what they perceive."

I should add here that the neurodivergent discomfort with eye contact would fall under sensory sensitivity, for me at least, and for some of the people I spoke to. It's not that it's physically challenging to look at people, as we don't inherently have vision issues. Eye contact isn't meant as a momentary action, though – what's prized is *sustained* eye contact, and that's where the struggle lies. I'm sure most of us are capable of moving our pupils into the eye-line of others, but to hold our gaze still in one place requires us not to be visually distracted by everything else happening outside of the people we're supposed to be looking at. It's so much easier for me to look around a room when trying to keep up with my fast-forwarded thoughts, but there are still people who view this as less than trustworthy, and given how many of us have experienced being seen as negligent, this obstacle is one that surely doesn't help our standing. It took me a decade and a half in the field to realize this, but part of the reason I like teaching and presenting so much is because you come off well by darting your eyes around the room at everyone else's for very brief periods – everyone appreciates the attention but isn't weirded out by being stared at. I played into my own strengths just by chance, so I got lucky, but that's not something that happens to all of us.

"I think for me," Ellie said, "the main thing I think of is the comfort factor if I would be wearing something. So I would like to wear pajamas a lot which again, just felt like a fun quirk, but I can look back and think like that would distract or bother me."

So that makes all three of the non-kitchen-based primary senses that have been given as examples. Ellie found a way to provide herself the necessary comfort, but not every school is going to allow you to show up in pajamas, and not every group of peers is going to allow you to show up in pajamas without teasing you. Additionally, physical touch extends to chairs and desks, most of which are hardly up to a teacher's discretion, so even a child whose standard school clothes aren't all that aggravating might find it hard to sit comfortably on what they've been provided, but again, without a diagnosis or an official accommodation, it's difficult to ask for a change. Even for the students who do have an IEP or something similar, being the kid with the Special Chair while not also having a highly visible condition can put an unwanted social target on your back.

Finally, Terry, whose sensitivity to light was brought up back in the very first chapter, told me about the ways that sensory issues have caused them strife throughout their studies:

> If somebody's tapping the back of my seat? That's highly problematic for me. Or repetitious noise that is not within my control. Or getting back to the physical things. If someone is sitting next to me and shaking their leg on the seat. It drives me insane like I have to get up and walk away. I just cannot. I can't be subjected to somebody else's mindless movement. I also don't like it when people are touching me in that way. If someone's like, rubbing my shoulder, and they're no longer thinking about it and they're just still doing it and it's in that like,

very repetitive way. It's very irritating to me. And so that's that's like the touch but also the same thing with sound. Loud noise I'm creating and in control of like, my loud music is fine, but other people's loud music is not okay. The temperature, like not being able to control the temperature around me, is also very problematic. I only can really be comfortable in a small range of tempera-ture. So if I don't have a door that I can shut where I can then control the temperature in my space, then I can get so uncomfortable, because my brain processes the wrong temperature as pain. When my fingers get cooled, they get stiff and they hurt and then I can't type or think.

There are a few things in this final excerpt I want to harp on briefly. First of all, the fact that one of the common themes here is the ability to control one's sensory environment, more so than needing complete silence or complete softness or what have you. When I asked to move to a new desk at my old job after telling them I had "sensory sensitivity," – *saying I had been diagnosed with ADHD felt too stigmatizing* – they did give me one, but the explan-ation for my new location was that it was "quiet." I didn't com-plain, even though quiet is not really what I need – I have lived within a few blocks of an above-ground train for several years and that's fine for me. It's not having to worry about sensory surprises that brings me the calm that helps me stay on track. Indeed, I wrote my entire college thesis with *Law and Order* – *the original, obviously* – playing in the background, because I was able to anticipate the rhythm of the episodes and knew nothing too auditorily chaotic was likely to occur.

Additionally, Terry mentions that it all settles into their body as pain when the discomfort can't be dealt with, but, as they explained, it's not as simple as "can't handle heat" or "can't handle cold," it's that there's a narrow band of comfort-able temperature. As a student who has likely already been painted as a disruptive nuisance, asking for a classroom to stay in a small range of degrees is not likely to go over well, espe-cially if the teacher has little control over the building's heating and cooling. It might even be perceived as making an excuse for poor performance, so we are likely to just try and grit our way through it until the bell rings.

We're not naive, though. None of us believe that it's possible for us to exist in fully controlled spaces at all times. As adults we can retreat to sensory comfort more often if we're privileged enough to have been able to build this into our lives and homes, but we know we're not in control of our classrooms, and that we're just one of however many differing levels of sensory sensitivities in the group. Sometimes all we know is that our chair just doesn't feel right, and when you're trying to deal with that sensation while also trying to remember what the teacher just said, *and* follow along as you take notes, *and* not skip any of the steps in the instructions you were just handed, I think you can see how these things pile up on each other like Jenga blocks just waiting to topple over.

Takeaways

You can really help us with this one, and not necessarily in the ways you might expect from having read through everyone's stories. Yes, please do whatever is within your power to be welcoming of the way we might choose to deal with our own sensory issues, be it informal attire or bright yellow sunglasses or earplugs or even, when appropriate, headphones for times when quiet work is happening. If a student wants to bring in a plush toy to squeeze to feel its softness, by all means let them do it. And sure, if someone is absent-mindedly making a repetitive noise, you can ask them to stop, but on the other hand, who's to say that the other student isn't also neurodivergent and clicking their pen as a means of getting their own pent-up energy out? The fact is, you're never going to be able to create perfect harmony between everyone's sensory needs at the same time, and it's not only neurodivergent students who have these sensitivities. But there's still plenty that can be done.

When the school year or semester starts, *ask students how they like to get their work done.* Ask them how they do their best work at home, what environments are most comfortable for them, and, if their home life doesn't meet these needs, what environments they would like to experience. For younger children, if more academic homework isn't yet a concern, you can make the discussion more elementary by asking more broadly about sounds, sights, and physical sensations that they like and dislike. The goal here is twofold: first, for those without the ability to fully articulate these sensitivities, providing a pathway towards a better understanding of themselves, and second, if you gather a list of these preferred environments, you can shift your approach to meet as many of the commonly cited contexts as possible, though you surely won't be able to do all of it at once.

You can also establish agreed upon signals for when students are either struggling with a sensation or, as Whitney mentioned, simply need a break. It could be a code word or a hand gesture or what have you, but, especially for us NDSOC who have experienced a great deal of shame for our traits, this might make it easier for us to feel comfortable expressing these needs before they become overwhelming. And yes, students could start "gaming the system" and taking breaks they don't "need," but who cares? The grace feels worth the risk given the possible benefit to so many, and you certainly don't have to be neurodivergent to benefit from the establishment of such a system. Maybe someone's just having a really emotional day and isn't in the right frame of mind to study – that student should have the space to process. But we'll get to the emotionality of the neurodivergent experience in a couple more chapters.

For now though, think about the students you've had who were anxious or upset for what seemed like no reason at all, and consider the possibility that there was, in fact, nothing wrong with them, no so-called maladaptive behavior, but just a chair that was a little too cold, a classroom that was a little too dimly lit, or someone whispering a few seats away. It looks irrational from the outside, and I'm not sure it's *rational* from the inside either, but it's certainly real, and sensory safety is a form of support that we need in order to be the best students we can be.

Notes

1   https://www.health.qld.gov.au/newsroom/features/sensory-overload-is-real-and-can-affect-any-combination-of-the-bodys-five-senses-learn-ways-to-deal-with-it. For more, see https://ca.specialisterne.com/sensory-safety-a-must-of-neurodiversity-inclusion-in-the-workplace/
2   Meier, S.M., Petersen, L., Schendel, D.E., Mattheisen, M., Mortensen, P.B., and Mors, O. (2015) Obsessive-Compulsive Disorder and Autism Spectrum Disorders: Longitudinal and Offspring Risk. *Plos One* 10 (11), e0141703. https://doi.org/10.1371/journal.pone.0141703

9

Trying to Catch the Express Train
On the Search for Hyperfocus

No, not quite done with the train references, but this is the chapter where it's the most relevant, because this time we're focused on . . . focus. Now, if the previous chapter was about something people tend to know about autism that happens to apply more broadly to the neurodivergent community, this one is more about something that basically everyone knows about ADHD that, it turns out, also applies more broadly to the neurodivergent community. It's right there in the name, after all.

One thing to note about the condition's official title is that there is a slash in it – it's technically "Attention Deficit/Hyperactivity Disorder," but, likely for convenience sake, people don't say the slash out loud. It may seem like I am being an erstwhile English teacher and focusing on punctuation, but the slash is important because it indicates that it can be either a deficit or hyperactivity, or it can be both. Similarly, when receiving an ADHD diagnosis, you can be classified as "inattentive" (essentially a stand-in for deficit), "hyperactive," or "combined," which, frankly, most of us are – I am. But the point I am making, though, is that the fact that most of us have occasions of hyperfocus, and can exhibit these at times in the classroom, makes it harder for people to take our moments of inattentiveness seriously. If we can do *that*,

DOI: 10.4324/9781003465126-10

people figure, something amazing and super-fast, then why can't we just stay on track the rest of the time? We must not care.

For autism, it's generally discussed more as a "special interest" that activates what I'll refer to in this chapter as hyperfocus, but regardless of what it's called, neurodivergent folks can vacillate between seemingly superhuman feats of concentration – to, as you'll see, a potentially unhealthy extent – and what seems from the outside to just be aimless daydreaming. This isn't to say we do not daydream – we surely do – but it's hardly aimless, and is a necessary counterbalance to the tunnel vision we can enter when we're, for lack of a better word, activated. Or, to fit this into the ongoing metaphor, when we're given the right tracks (that is, supportive contexts), we can basically magnetically levitate – *the process that the world's fastest trains, mostly in Japan, use to travel hundreds of miles per hour* – and when we're not, we can absolutely derail or even crash.

With all that said, though, by this point in the book, it should be clearer that we're not just choosing not to pay attention or being careless with our time. Not only are our neurotypes out of our control, but there's also all the other traits you've heard about thus far that can gum up the works and make it impossible to stay on track. Without a diagnosis, and with the identities that we have, we receive those supportive contexts much less often and are often blamed when things fall apart. So, in this chapter, you'll hear what the wild swings between zero focus and hyperfocus look like from the outside and feel like from the inside, and also how you might be able to help us find our tracks.

Counter-Narratives

The first time I recall my hyperfocus fully kicking in in a way that helped me academically was when I was on a very uncomfortable several-hour bus ride at the end of eighth grade. It wasn't a bus ride that was a part of my school day, but actually a Memorial Day trip to a massive Boy Scout complex somewhere in upstate New York. Yes, I was a Boy Scout, and though I eventually soured on the organization for reasons I'm sure you're aware of if you follow the news, at the start, it was a lot of fun, and I got closer to my stepdad because of his interest in camping and rafting and other outdoorsy stuff. I was into it, basically, until I realized that the Friday night meetings and weekend trips meant I couldn't really do any socializing as I entered my teens, but then it's not like I was invited to the parties much anyway.

In eighth grade, I'd made enough, uh, Boy Scout progress that I was being inducted into something called The Order of the Arrow, which, I don't even remember anymore but it was important and in order (ha) to join you had to endure a long weekend where you weren't allowed to speak. You also had to sleep outside on the ground the first night without even the protection of a tent. Look, I don't know, man. But I was not looking forward to any of it, especially because I, as ever, struggled to socialize with a lot of the other scouts and I *wasn't allowed to speak*.

To try and take my mind off of what was ahead of me, when I sat down on the bus, I pulled out my assigned English book, which was a memoir called *This Boy's Life*, by Tobias Wolff, which I had no idea was a DiCaprio/De Niro movie. I probably had about 40 pages assigned over the weekend, and I got to work reading it, when an amazing thing happened that I'd never felt before. I guess it was something about the book being centered on a character fairly close to my age and the engaging prose – *I'm reluctant to go back and verify if this is actually true* – but I read those 40 pages and I just kept going. I kept going for the entire ride, I kept going until the sun set and I had to use my flashlight to read. I kept going until I was literally walking down off the bus and they made me stop, and I finished the last few pages the following day. This left me with an extremely dull several-hour ride back since it was the only book I'd brought and we got stuck in holiday-weekend traffic, but as far as the negative consequences of hyperfocus go, it wasn't that bad. More importantly, when I walked into English class the next week, I could hardly contain my glee at being ahead of all my classmates. My English teacher had to keep reminding me not to say what happened in later chapters, so I mostly sat in my chair with joy until everyone else caught up weeks later. This was the start of my understanding that getting really far ahead was a lot more fun than trying not to fall behind, and I continue it to this day. But in order to be days, weeks, months ahead, you have to tap into that hyperfocus, and it took me years to figure out how to access it voluntarily, and my educators never quite figured out how to help me find it, with the exception of a few very special teachers.

Terry gave me a detailed description of their lifelong history of, and skill with, tapping into that hyperfocus:

> As far as I can remember, I have been able to lose myself in a book. I think it had to do with needing to dissociate from the environment that I was in because every-thing around me was so controlled. My parents were extremely controlling, and I wasn't really allowed to leave the house. And so I hyperfocused on books from an early age. I could read a newspaper at bedtime when I was four. As I said, I had a hyperlexic IQ. And so you're reading Stephen King in high school. I was reading 1000-page books when I was like eight years old. I was reading *The Power of Positive Thinking* and *I'm Okay, You're Okay*. And you know, *The Naked Ape*. When I was still in pri-mary school, I was reading books that adults read. And I was reading a lot, because if I didn't, I had to do chores, or I had to play with my brother who was problematic for other reasons. So I hyperfocused constantly when I was in high school. My dad made me create a study schedule that was 24 hours a week outside of school, from age 14 to 16. And then that went up to 40 hours a week outside of school and homework from age 16 to 18. And so, what I would do, because I couldn't do school like normal kids . . . So I was just really interested in everything, had encyclopedias at home, and I would study everything in my textbooks, but I would focus on a chapter that was of interest to me. So if there were 20 chapters in the book, I might start off with chapter 13, because that's interesting. Read that whole chapter. Learn everything in it. After reading it maybe three times and then go on to the next

chapter. I was really interested in Shakespeare and I read *Macbeth* so many times that I memorized the whole thing. Without trying, I just noticed by the time I started doing it a third time that I already knew every word as I was going through it. So I've been hyperfocusing like this my entire life.

If you weren't familiar with how we think by now, you might see all of that as bragging, while at the same time feeling the familiar frustration we've experienced from educators when we can't accomplish something seemingly simple. There is one very short key phrase in all that detail that sums it all up. Can you find it? It's in the second-to-last sentence. Right.

"Without trying."

When we're on, it feels like it takes no effort at all to swallow a book whole or, relevant for me, to write one. It's similar to the concept of "flow," as coined by Mihaly Csikszentmihalyi,[1] which he defines accordingly, as excerpted by *Positive Psychology*:[2]

1. Complete concentration;
2. Clarity of goals and reward in mind and immediate feedback;
3. Transformation of time (speeding up/slowing down);
4. The experience is intrinsically rewarding;
5. Effortlessness and ease;
6. There is a balance between challenge and skills;
7. Actions and awareness are merged, losing self-conscious rumination;
8. There is a feeling of control over the task.

Well, that sure doesn't sound like the stereotypes of neurodivergent kids, or even the stories you've heard in this book thus far. Csikszentmihalyi posits that flow is the key to happiness. I'm not necessarily sure about all of *that*, but I can tell you there's absolutely no better feeling, you don't have to contend with any anxiety whatsoever, and you get a rush of what has to be endorphins. Time really does seem to slow way down when I'm on the express train in my brain. Every time I have a task ahead of me, I try and think of ways to access the feeling that hyperfocus provides, and though it eludes me much of the time, the occasions when it occurs are transcendent.

Terry had more to say that was about their adulthood and current life, and in the second half of what they shared, you should start see why this might become a problem in a traditional classroom:

> I just have always been hyperfocusing on whatever was interesting to me at the time. So my dad gave me a camera. I took tons of photographs of my friends, I would organize a fashion show. And like, I just would come up with an idea and follow through on it in this hyperfocused way, and so I just did a bunch of different things. I taught myself how to play the Venezuelan cuatro in 2017. And every day for over a year, I would practice until I got to the point where now I'm self-taught on this instrument. Right now for me what my hyperfocus tends to be is things about anything that's sort of socio-cultural, sort of connected to racism, sexism, neurodivergence, body positivity, sex positivity, so I do a lot of writing in those areas. I help with throwing different events. I do a lot of event production with my friends. I do a lot of costuming. I do occasional performances, I am constantly promoting my friends' events, creating media, using the journey to create the images. I hyperfocus on my journey for hours and hours and you know, like to the point where sometimes I'll be like going to the bathroom and I'm like sitting on the toilet still generating images and posting things and you know, I can also hyperfocus sometimes on food, so I will go and buy a bunch of ingredients that are for Trinidadian recipes, and then I'll spend hours and hours in the kitchen at my friend's place, making food for them. You know, I get really depressed when the hyperfocus goes away. And that's usually because I am alone. And I don't have a human being around me to sort of like pull me out of my sort of catatonic state of not having enough dopamine to do anything. But as soon

as someone walks in the door, they can generate some kind of hyperfocus out of me. Either I immediately start telling them a really long story, or I sprang into action and I start cleaning things around my apartment. Or if they're coming for dinner, I will immediately start making food and I can just hyperfocus on making that food for hours in a row.

The problems, as far as some schools are concerned, start right in the first sentence. Whatever interests us *at the time* is not exactly what we're told to study in school. I suspect that part of the reason so many of us just keep going back to school is because, the farther you go into advanced degrees, the more you do get to study whatever interests you. After all, what's a doctorate if not precisely what you're obsessed with? When I read all of that, I see a brilliant and creative autodidact to be cherished, but if you're just standing in front of them, hoping they'll follow along with your lesson when they're thinking about one of their special interests, and you don't actually know why because of a lack of diagnosis or guidance, then yeah, it just might get on your nerves.

"It's always been easier to pay attention to things that I'm interested in," Rose told me. "And I think it was easier for me to bridge the gaps when I had more fear-based motivators in my life," she added, chuckling a little. "I probably shouldn't be laughing at that.

"I think it's very hard and it's gotten harder as time has gone on to regulate my attention," she continued. "I like science. I like poetry and I'm very sentimental and like, I run into this problem of like, if I don't like micromanage the hell out of myself or take medication, all of a sudden I'm spending the whole day chasing butterflies. And you think that that will get better as I get older. It's actually worse, I think. I'm trying to figure that out."

There is a bit of an archaic perception that people will "grow out" of certain neurodivergent traits, which is not true, but can seem true if, as adults, we're able to place ourselves in situations that better meet our needs. For example, I don't feel the need to wear my earplugs when I'm around people I'm completely comfortable with, not because my sensitivities have vanished but because they're harder to manage when I'm worried how I'll be perceived.

Ellie's story begins to hint at the ways that hyperfocus can be activated. "I definitely relate to the hyperfocus thing. I think I would like do something like have a paper due," she said, "but I would do it for like seven hours in a row. Or something like not at all and then it's right before it's due and like boom, huge, like sustained effort. And I think I would always be like, 'wow, this is so cool. Like other people can't do this, but I can do this.' I never noticed that it wasn't the style that my peers would work in.

"I have this other mode," she continued. "The TV was always on in my house. And even there were multiple TVs and I think just like with my family it was like we were always together. You didn't really go be in your room alone or something. And so I would work while there was TV on and you know, conversation, all types of stuff going. And I think sometimes that would allow me to work for longer because I was only partially working like there was a little bit of my brain would go to homework and a little bit would go to that."

What she's hinting at is something I've experienced, and something I described in the previous chapter. It's rare that complete silence or a total lack of sensory stimulation will allow us to reach hyperfocus, because our brains will wander towards, as Rose says, chasing butterflies. If we can employ a familiar sensation to occupy the part of our brain that wants to daydream, and we're interested in what's in front of us, then we can get to the state we need to be in to do what only we can really do.

Robyn reflected on the way summative assessments were often not a great way for her to tap into her focus. "Giving me one assignment for the semester was a set up for a poor performance," she explained. "I might be successful in the performance at the end. But I needed more bite-sized engagements to, like you said, schedule small bursts of productivity as opposed to you know, trying to expect me to pace myself if you leave it to me. Um, but, ya know, I'm not as I'm not as good at predicting it or setting the stage for it." She's being modest, given how far she's gotten in her career, but that's the issue: just like work, school is often a series of tasks that don't necessarily align with where our brain wants to be, and to try and push ourselves through that is an absolute slog. We can sometimes do it, eventually, but it won't be our best work. Yet school can't possibly cater to our every whim.

And then there's the fact that hyperfocus itself, while fun and freeing while it lasts, can leave us hollowed out, feeling empty the way Terry described. When the express train stops and we have to wait for the next one, the delay can be interminable. More than just being impatient, though, this can actually have serious consequences for us. Marie put it plainly in describing how she hit a wall and basically gave up:

> People viewed [hyperfocusing] as a good thing when in my head it was actually kind of self-destructive. Like it led me to not rest properly ever. And I remember my senior year of high school, I was beyond burned out, I cried almost every day. Granted there are a lot of circumstances. I had a pretty rough senior year of high school, my favorite teacher who was my choir teacher passed away. And there was a lot going on personally, just with the stress of trying to get scholarships, so I didn't have a great senior year, but I cried every single day for a very long period of time, but it's because I was really emotionally dysregulated because I was hyperfocusing on either getting my homework done or filling out a scholarship application. And the teachers didn't really do or say anything because they didn't think there was any-thing wrong with getting my stuff done, and that's what mattered to them. Um, so I do remember at one point, my senior year, my principal called me into the office and was like, you know, we've noticed you really don't want to be here and I was like, listen and I said this straight up. I said, 'I'm only here because I'm legally required to be here. Otherwise, I would not be here.' And I think it shocked them that I said that. But to me, I was like, I have done all my homework. I have done all my scholarship applications. And now I'm still forced to show up for

eight hours of nonsense that I don't care about . . . And so I think I think it was really nice that they expressed that concern for me, but they still didn't fully understand what the root of the problem was. And the root of the problem is that I was emotionally dysregulated and being forced to sit in an environment that made it worse. You know, instead of saying okay, maybe she just needs like, a study hall where she can sit there and be calm or like if I'm napping in class, why are we being mad at me for napping instead of questioning why I need to nap in class? You know, because I was never that student until my senior year. And then it got to the point where I was so drained and so exhausted that I would just when the teacher was done talking, I was out.

Takeaways

The challenge here is how to help us find our hyperfocus but not run ourselves into the ground while doing so, especially at ages where we probably haven't figured out a system that works best for us to both get our work done and take care of ourselves. When Rose gained a better understanding of herself post-diagnosis and as she worked through graduate school, she had to start forgiving herself for her desire to chase butterflies. "I think one of the most valuable and important things that I've done is to learn love and compassion and grace for myself," she said, "because, you know, even if I am frustrated, I think it's just sort of foundational, fundamental. Not to sort of attack myself for that. It's important for sustainability." But again, we all had to figure these things out ourselves and my hope is that teachers reading this can help guide us towards this earlier in our lives so we don't have to risk experiences like the one Marie shared above.

So, the first important thing is, especially for younger students, to help us find our way to hyperfocus/flow by *closely observing, and taking explicit note of, the environments in which we seem to take off like rockets. Even if it's just short bursts of extra academic energy, write it down somewhere, because maybe you can create that context again when we might seem to be stuck and help us tap into the super speed.*

Once we've found our way to hyperfocus, either with your help or by ourselves, *do whatever you can to, as the saying goes, let us cook (i.e., get out of the way).* My best educational experience came in my doctoral program because everyone eventually figured out it was best not to interfere when I was on a roll and that's how I finished so quickly. If that means letting a student keep working on a particular assignment when the class has moved on, or giving them grace if they arrive slightly late because they were hyperfocusing, please do it.

But, the flipside of this is helping us avoid the crash. We generally do not like to be interrupted when we're On One, but *if you reiterate for the class that you are likely to check in with us to see if we're pacing ourselves, then it won't come as a huge disruption, and we might actually let you help us take care of ourselves.*

At this point in my life and career, my reputation has done a complete 180 from the way my teachers used to look at me as someone who never followed through on his assignments and obligations, and I'm one of the people at work who's known for Getting Things Done early and effectively, yet I have found my way to the balance I lacked for the first 20 years I was hyperfocusing. The express train in my brain helped me write this last part very quickly, but the train started wobbling during the last paragraph and I had to stand up and sit back down to make it to the station. I shouldn't have to have gotten a whole doctorate to figure out those tricks, but I think these suggestions will help you help us stay on track.

Notes

1 Csikszentmihalyi, M. (2002) *Flow: The Psychology of Happiness: The Classic Work on How to Achieve Happiness.* London: Rider.
2 https://positivepsychology.com/mihaly-csikszentmihalyi-father-of-flow/

10

Catching Our Breath
On Emotional Volatility

People tend to think of neurodivergence as purely psychological, in both a negative and positive sense. There have been a few chapters thus far that attempted to paint a more detailed picture of our other common traits, including some that are more tangible and physical (e.g., sensory sensitivities). But if you take one new thing away from this book, both from the information about neurodivergence in general and the particular realities of said experience while also being a student of color, it should probably be this: the neurodivergent life is a deeply emotional one, and the lack of tools we are provided with to handle these feelings contributes substantially to the difficulties we face in the classroom.

There's certainly a biological aspect to this emotionality. "Challenges with emotions start in the brain itself," wrote Dr. Thomas Brown. "Sometimes the working memory impairments of ADHD allow a momentary emotion to become too strong, flooding the brain with one intense emotion."[1] Later in the same article, he repeats the same phrasing, describing these moments as emotional "floods," "a momentary emotion that can gobble up all of the space in his head just like a computer bug can gobble up all of the space on a hard drive." It's hard

DOI: 10.4324/9781003465126-11

enough to deal with that in my late 30s, so imagine trying to process that as a child, or, even worse, during puberty, when hormones are going haywire for even the "typical" adolescent. In fact, it can be hard to distinguish a more standard hormonal reaction from what might be exacerbated by undiagnosed neurodivergence.

Some of the language in that article describing these emotionalities verges on stigmatizing, though, even from an expert who is nominally trying to support us. See if you can understand what I mean by that in the following statement:

> The brain's gating mechanism for regulating emotion does not distinguish between dangerous threats and more minor problems. These individuals are often thrown into panic mode by thoughts or perceptions that do not warrant such a reaction.

Well, who decides what does and doesn't "warrant such a reaction?" I can see how someone watching us in the class-room might observe an emotional outburst and decide that it's extreme for the situation, yet without knowing the many other times we've felt dismissed or criticized, it would be difficult to understand why tears or anger are actually perfectly rational. Even in sharing my own stories from earlier chapters, a part of me worries that readers may see those as minor and wonder why they had such a lasting effect on me, but they hit me like an anvil at the time.

Emotions are inherently subjective and irrational, after all, but the real trouble comes in when we're not allowed to express these feelings because they're too inconvenient for others, and because, since we are classified as exceptions in several senses, we "should" be able to handle things without getting upset. This chapter and the two that follow are centered on aspects of our emotionality, and will hopefully provide some insight into behaviors you might have witnessed from students of yours that you might have thought were Too Much or over the top or dramatic or what have you. I assure you, for us, the reactions are warranted. But even if you're not a trained counselor or someone with that sort of role, I do believe you can help us deal with what we feel when we're in your classroom.

Counter-Narratives

Long after I'd figured out how to access hyperfocus and started doing my homework as early as possible, I found myself with an academic nemesis I hinted at earlier: calculus. Like I said, it didn't make sense to me when math got theoretical. I am perfectly comfortable with theory in the sense of scholarship because that really just means a prism through which you can analyze a phenomenon, but I couldn't do calculus at all. The thing is, not only had I skipped first grade, but then, in fourth grade, they'd decided that fourth grade math was too easy for me, so I got skipped an additional level in that subject. So, from the age of eight, I was in math classes with people more than two years my senior. And I kept up with it, outpaced them really, until I got to the more advanced math when I was in high school. I say all this to say that I was always noticeably smaller and less mature than my math classmates, and I was acutely aware of this, and the expectations that were placed on me to continue to stay near the top of the class.

One day, it finally all came tumbling down when, no matter how hard I tried to concentrate, I couldn't figure out any of the questions on a unit exam. Although most of my white classmates who had diagnoses for what was at the time just called ADD were given extra time to take tests, I always flew through any sort of standardized assessment and usually walked out of the room early when my teachers would get annoyed at my fidgeting. I walked out of my SAT long before the time limit was over because I was confident I'd done well, and I had. And many, many years later, I did the same thing when I took the GRE, which, annoyingly, had geometry on it. But anyway, on that day in calculus class, I saw other people finishing before me and leaving the room, I watched the time tick off the analog clock, the teacher gave us reminders that we needed to finish up, and I just got out of my chair, leaned against the wall and cried. No one was mean to me this time, certainly not the teacher, and in fact people expressed a mix of concern and confusion. Everyone, including me, chalked it up to general disappointment at not doing well on the test, but looking back, it was a moment where one of the most important parts of my adolescent identity – my status as a testing dynamo – was falling to pieces, and feelings of intense shame and embarrassment were washing over me.

The teacher, a sunny young woman I'll call Ms. Brooks, offered to spend extra time tutoring me on the topic, which I tried to refuse but then, fearing another future meltdown, I agreed, and we spent a few afternoons in the hallway outside of her office going over things that I never fully understood. I wasn't a super "cool" kid, obviously, but I could always count on being seen as "smart," so now I was one of the students you would walk by and see them getting extra help, and I did not like the feeling one bit. Obviously, there's nothing wrong with needing extra support – that's what this whole book is about after all – but because of how little I'd received to that point, I was conditioned to handle everything myself, and at that moment, and at a few others, it just became way too much. Whether or not I agree with how Dr. Brown phrased everything in his article, I was definitely being "flooded" and I could not keep my head above the surface.

Terry told me about the ways they weren't believed or supported when their emotions became visible, from adolescence up through continued reverberations in her career. As ever, they were insightful about the way their identity impacted their treatment:

> I definitely have extreme emotions, and they last longer than other people's emotions. And I was not believed when I was a child, people around me, my mother in particular, they believed that I was exaggerating how I felt. I was accused of having crocodile tears because I had an emotion and I cried and they thought I was doing it for attention. And I feel like this also happens in the workplace as well, that particularly white women think that I am using my tears as ways to manipulate and the reality

is that when you are a Black person and have spent your entire life having your emotions, dismissed, been ignored by other people, I'm being punished for having emotions, that the fact that in the workplace you are unable to hold back tears. That is not an attempt of manipulation. That is an inability to control the physical response of your body to emotions and they don't view it that way. So it becomes an additional thing that is held against you . . . When I was a child, I once got kicked out of my math class, because at age 11 I wasn't able to hold back tears when I couldn't figure out some math problem and my teacher was actually a distant relative of mine, who had zero empathy for me in that situation, and asked me to leave the classroom. And so and it's the same thing that's been happening to me essentially my whole life from people who should have had some amount of empathy for me.

Hmm, that math class story sounds somewhat familiar. Anyway, in a separate conversation I had with a white neurodivergent friend named Kimberly, she told me that she also cries often, and that although her father has occasionally expressed frustration that she was visibly emotional, no educator has ever accused her of being manipulative or deceitful. "It's also just more socially acceptable for white women to cry," she said. This book is focused on the voices of people of color, but I thought it was important to hear a concurrence from someone who had similar traits but different treatment. As I said way back in the Introduction, there is no biological difference between our brains and those of white neurodivergent students, but what we're allowed to do and express is shaped by the place we occupy in society.

"Black and brown kids are not given the latitude to, you know, have the traditional Attention Deficit Disorder, hyperactivity and stuff like that," Robyn told me. "It just tends not to be acceptable. And yeah, it's, it's challenging because I think growing up, you know, our symptoms and our situations are not not really validated."

"This is a part of my life where I don't know where I have actual anxiety or if the ADHD created the anxiety," Rachel explained. "It's impossible [to tell]. But I think you know, when it came to those things, I was so in my head about making all of my points that I would ramble on. It's the same thing even with like today, like you might understand this with the podcasting to like, I just want to make my points but I ended up not making my points. Maybe I go on a tangent and then I forget about one of my points. But that would happen when I'd have to do presentations and I think or do some sort of recap. And, you know, a lot of times they don't want you to use note cards or anything for your presentations, like any sort of help there. Because you know, and my short-term memory again, I just couldn't do presentations on the fly or just, I mean, it's about emotional regulation. I was a mess anytime I knew that I had to do a presentation and because I knew all this anxiety would come up and bite me in the ass." (Both Rachel and I host podcasts. Mine's called *Unstandardized English*. I won't tell you who she is, but she's been on my show before.)

Having your emotions diminished or dismissed does not have the desired effect of actually curtailing these feelings but can only have a few possible results, none of which are positive: we stifle these impulses as best we can and end up having more explosive outbursts at truly inopportune times, or we just try and dissociate from ourselves and don't let ourselves actually feel anything. I mostly chose the latter path after the former led to scenes like the math class meltdown. I told you however many pages ago that I didn't let myself cry for something like a dozen years, and the impetus for this full emotional shutdown was being teased for being visibly emotional at a party my freshman year in college, when I just felt lonely and was unable to hide it. One student did ask me if I was okay, which was enough of a push to get me to extricate myself from the situation, but the damage was done. *Never again,* I told myself, and if I'd never met my wife, that might still be true, because the only thing that got me to feel my feelings again was meeting and loving her.

Whitney chose the other option, shutting everything away and then exploding:

I was very overly emotional. My brothers and dad would say like, 'You're just emotional. You're just sensitive,' which would upset me even more. I'm like, 'I'm not trying to be overly emotional or sensitive about things.' I don't have a memory of getting upset and crying or anything like that at school. I think I would have been more embarrassed so I really, it's not like healthy, but I would stuff that down until I got home. And I would hide my emotion in some ways and but not always at home, but I'm just more saying like there's no instance at school where I remember like, visibly getting upset, I think if anything I was more quote unquote angry to people and like, there were times I would like snap on people or like, you know, show my aggression towards them especially like stupid boys. That would be annoying to me. I would say if anything, I displayed more anger at school, which is kind of shocking in some ways. But I think it was because I was overwhelmed and also very sensitive. But at home I cried a lot, all the time. And even as an adult often there are times that there are certain things that will upset me that shouldn't really upset me but my reaction is to cry or to be like overwhelmed in that way.

I will be honest with all of you and say that these conversations I had with all of them were actually really fun and validating, but the more I read through the transcripts as I re-assemble them into chapters and broader narratives, it all makes me pretty sad. Even what Whitney said of herself at the end there – "certain things that will upset me that shouldn't really upset me" – implies that we are poor judges of what is and isn't appropriate and that the societal measurements for "correct" emotionality are what we should rely on. In this chapter, I want to make the point that there are few people who would be able to feel what's happening in our brains and not react very strongly. But even if we're never told this explicitly, we all know that if we act "the wrong way," folks like us will end up suspended, expelled, arrested, imprisoned, dead. That may seem stark, but, whether it's a special level of talent or, more likely, talents that happened to align better with academic expectations than those of others, we were able to pull through to the other side and reach enough stability to have these reflective discussions. So many of us can't swallow the emotions, either because their life is so challenging that their ability to do so is compromised or because their version of neurodivergence is more, shall we say, intense. We all ended up with scars that may never fully heal because of how we had to fight our own brains, and I say to you that we should be told that what we feel is valid and legitimate, and be given tools to process these feelings, instead of told, either explicitly or by implication, that what we're feeling is The Wrong Way To Feel.

Marie either wasn't afraid to show her emotions or didn't have the ability to stop them. Whichever of these was true, she wore her heart, and her tears, on her sleeve, and it wasn't always something that was supported in her school experience:

> I was a crier, and I wasn't afraid to cry in public because to me, like, if I have an emotion, I'm not necessarily going to hide it, but there were moments where people tried to shame me for that. It's not like I was disruptively crying. I was often just kind of sitting there in my little bubble like crying it out a little, because I knew that if I cried it out a little I could get over it. Like I just needed that emotional release and then I could keep going after I had maybe five to 10 minutes of just like sitting there overwhelmed and flustered. But you know, when you only have a 50-minute class period, and you take five minutes of that to cry over your homework, it's not viewed very positively by your teachers. So a lot of times I would try to let it out on my breaks. I think back to my senior year, because I would be walking down the hallway crying, everyone was like, 'Oh my God, what's wrong with her?' And I of course appreciate the concern, you know, but at the same time, it was like I was trying to regulate and the only way that I knew how, and that was by letting it out, you know, and it's not like my emotional outlet growing up was singing, and so it's not like I could sing in the middle of an exam.

I mean, maybe we should be allowed to sing during our exams. I bet some people would enjoy hearing it. But anyway, the 'what's wrong with her?' moment is the key of this topic for us. There's seemingly a short list of acceptable reasons for a non-toddler to cry, and I encourage everyone reading this to blow up this list in their heads. I still don't exactly cry very often, the muscles are weak after a decade of shutting them off, but people can show deep emotion for any reason, and it's not necessarily an emergency or a reason to think there's something wrong with that person. Oh, sure, there might be something wrong with their day or their life that's making things hard for them, but for folks like us, it often gets attached to us as people, and that reputation for supposedly excessive emotionality can be hard to shake.

Speaking of something being wrong with a person's life, Ellie shared her insight that, after going through a very tough stretch with her family, she did what she could to make certain people didn't get a glimpse of how she truly felt. "It was such a time marked by crisis and struggle and I remember crying a lot," she told me. "I couldn't let my family see that I was struggling but then I think the other times I was like, so happy, like, happier than other people, but I thought that was cool. So I'm not sure what could have been done better. But at the same time, I think it's kind of sad that I had all those experiences and I really didn't start to get any emotional tools or anything like that until I was like a full grown adult.

"I feel like there is that element of kids of color, in all likelihood having just like more shit going down," she continued, "and I don't really feel like there was any specific mechanisms in place to like, be supportive around that stuff other than I think peers was the only place I really looked to, but then sometimes your peers are not really mature enough to be helpful."

It's great if you happen to have good friends that will help you through these things, but not only are they not professionals, they are also not adults, and there's only so much they can do for us.

Finally, Rose explained, similarly to Ellie, that her home life had contributed to her emotional reality, and that, after a certain point, it became too much to suppress. "I've always had way too many emotions and a lot of strong emotions," she said. "There were a lot of ways that I wasn't allowed to express my emotions and I think you know, having a parent that also had some emotional dysregulation and very clearly had a bad temper, and I know that I kind of had that same thing. But for me, it was like, you know, not learning strategies. To not trigger more . . . And I think, you know, to me, that definitely influenced the way I acted at school. Sort of this fear of authority just shaped my interactions and changed the way that I would operate and express things but at a point it kind of like I don't know, just eventually spilled over."

It's probably not great that I keep calling out the people I interviewed, but there's so much self-judgment in everything they're saying that I want to keep highlighting it to ensure that readers know what can happen if teachers and school don't step in while this is going on. All I have to say for now is that there is no such thing as "too many emotions," and trying to stop them is both ineffective and deeply harmful.

Takeaways

This one is tough, you know? You're not medical professionals. You're probably not trained as counselors. How can you even tell if someone is dealing with puberty or dealing with neurodivergence . . . or both?

I say to you, it doesn't matter why. Especially since we're not likely to be diagnosed, you're probably never going to know. What I propose here should be useful for any students of color who have rarely been given ownership of their own emotions.

Marie told a story about a meltdown she had in math class – that subject sure does keep coming up! – and a memorable way her school responded to it:

> I spent about an hour working on the exam and it still was not coming to me. I just couldn't remember how to do it. And so I turned it in half-blank and [my teacher] said she had never seen a student shut down like that and

I think that's what prompted the principal to call me into his office because she was so worried about me after I just like stopped because she was like, 'That's not like her to just hit a wall and quit,' but I completely gave up. I mean, what was I going to do just like magically know how to do it? In my head I just gave up because I just didn't know how to do it, you know, but in her head she could see like the deeper issues going on with that like something else is happening here. And [Marie] is hitting a wall. So I hit this wall, and I turned in the exam half-blank and I mean I was grateful because I still was able to pass the class. She gave me a lot of extra credit at that point. But she said that she went to the office and was like, 'I'm failing her as a teacher.' And to me it was like a teacher that like actually took it that seriously, my emotion, so it kind of almost made me feel guilty for having those emotions because I didn't want her to feel like a failure, because she wasn't failing, it was just a matter of like, I forgot how to do something on a test at a really emotionally dysregulated point in my life. And you know, it was great that she did care because I needed someone to care at that point. But I will never forget that.

I'm not saying you have to prostrate yourself in front of your students and administrators and admit you are an abject failure. I've already mentioned the value of vulnerability. But more specifically, when it comes to the intersection between our emotions and identities, *please reassure us that whatever emotion we're showing is okay*. I didn't say all behavior is okay – you should stop someone from violence, obviously – but we've been told that being upset, even in a non-disruptive way, is nonetheless shameful, and we need to be reminded that that isn't true.

Rachel suggested letting us use whatever support tools we might have developed for our emotions, but I will go one step further and say *spend some time asking people what makes them feel emotionally safe*. Some students might laugh, but if you're a teacher and afraid of being laughed at, I don't know what to tell you; they've been laughing at me for 16 years. Whatever people choose to share, there's only so much you can practically implement, but even the effort will show us that we're supported in some small way.

Ultimately, most of this emotional work is not your responsibility, and I do want to be clear about that. With that said, though, however many years most of us have spent in therapy, it's not your job to replace that, but moments like the one Marie described, moments like Ms. Brooks checking in on me despite my resistance, moments where we don't think we're "crazy" for feelings we can't control, we never forget them, so create as many of those moments as you can.

Note

1 See https://www.additudemag.com/slideshows/adhd-emotions-under standing-intense-feelings/ for more.

11

Being an Easy Target
On the Persistent Perception of Social Rejection

The thing about all of these traits we tend to share is that, much as some of the people interviewed spoke about trying to stay out of view, we still get noticed for being different from other kids. And, especially if we *look* different from our classmates on top of it, we tend to stand out, for better or worse. As you know by now, we experience our emotions very strongly, and then those reactions call even more attention to us, and, for a lot of us, social rejection, or really the perception thereof, can be exceptionally painful.

There's something called "rejection sensitive dysphoria," which you can probably figure out the meaning of from the name, but, here is a description from a clinical social worker named Melissa Nunes-Harwin:

> The thoughts that accompany rejection sensitivity can be intense and extreme. A boss giving feedback on your work may lead to fears of being fired; a friend turning down an invitation could make you wonder if you're being kicked out of the social group. "We need to talk" are words that send you into a downwards spiral. Some

DOI: 10.4324/9781003465126-12

people describe the sensation of rejection sensitivity as being as bad or worse as physical pain.[1]

It's not something you can be officially diagnosed with, but then, neither is neurodivergence itself as a broader category, but what matters is that it's real for many of us, and is particularly common in our community. It's an insidious, corrosive feeling that you can't really argue your way out of with a list of facts. No matter how well many of us do in school or at work, the perception of rejection can follow us around our entire lives. And yes, the "solution" to this is obviously professional help, but if these thoughts start long before we have any diagnosis or are seen as needing treatment, we can struggle our way through years of painful rumination to the point that it can deeply hinder our performance at school and work and can be ruinous to interpersonal relationships. And then, with those relationships rendered fragile or non-existent, the isolation that follows exacerbates all of the other traits you've been reading about thus far. It honestly took me until I got to add a Dr. to my name, published a book, *and* got a more supportive job – all of which happened within a few dizzying months in 2022 – before I finally fully believed I would not be rejected by new groups of people, and I still put in my earplugs to stay calm when I'm in an unfamiliar social environment. I'm glad I'm mostly past it, but that's a lot of work to have to do to get to this point, and I obviously hadn't done any of it when I was an adolescent.

Counter-Narratives

"I think all of that was because I felt like I was so different and like, everyone's going to reject me," Whitney told me. "I just thought people would reject me already. So I definitely was feeling that and yeah, I don't know. I really didn't overcome that in some ways until I was like 25 or 27. Realistically, like sometimes I still feel it, but I think I have a better handle or control on it. But yeah, I think a lot of what I was doing was because I was acting from the perception already that people think I'm weird. People think

I'm different. People don't want to be around me or like don't understand me. That was a big thing. I would always tell myself that people don't understand me. But I think it's because I also didn't understand all of the things that were going on with me. So you know, I was labeling myself too."

Whitney's reflection here exemplifies the internal battle many of us undergo, projecting rejection onto others before they've actually done so. Or sometimes, a rare moment of genuine rejection – because it happens to everyone occasionally – is held onto for a very long time and just festers into anxiety and fear. As soon as someone calls you "weird," or "annoying," – or "irksome" – that's who you think you are forever, or at least until you mature enough to disentangle these thoughts either by yourself or with professional help.

"I literally feel like I hyperfocused on making friends in college because I wanted to have those connections that everyone leaving high school had," Whitney explained. "You know, like, 'these are my best friends forever.' And there are people that I know from high school that I still talk to, but I was just like, I don't have any friends. And like that doesn't feel good. So I really did focus a lot on joining clubs and like, again, I think that was a way like I wasn't paying attention in the classroom. Then I was hyperfocusing on what needed to be done for this organization that I joined, which like, *was* important, but also, not my job. And I was making it almost a job hyperfixating on what to do to make this a more enjoyable experience. And yeah, that wasn't what I should have been doing with my time."

When Whitney told me this it helped me reach a revelation about my own experience. When I wrote in a previous chapter about that evening I read the whole book on the bus ride, I mentioned that that was the first time I could remember hyperfocusing in a way that was school-related. What I mean is, up to that point, I did occasionally hyperfocus, but only on my various random interests, including all the train trivia I keep sharing, and these things weren't exactly on the curriculum. So when Whitney said this, I realized that the same thing was true of me: all my hyperfocus energy at school was trained on trying to be accepted by my peers, failing, trying again, and failing again, and, just like she said, it's why, aside from being good at tests, I was never a standout student relative to my peers until I was well into adulthood. Even in my doc program, I was worried my classmates would think I was weird and wouldn't like me, but, as far as I can tell, almost everyone in that program respected me, and it was a strange and confusing feeling.

And to be clear, I *am* weird, and so is Whitney, who has become a close friend of mine – it's just that that shouldn't be a bad word. Every single children's book and film seems to have the message that it's okay to be yourself, yet there's still a limit to how different you're allowed to be, and most of us fell just on the other side of that line and paid the psychological price for it.

Rachel told me about how her anxiety about her friend's decision to spend time with someone else occupied her focus when she, also, could have been studying:

> I remember being so worried about whether or not my friend would be able to spend the night on the weekend or if she were going to be spending the night with someone else. And did that mean that she didn't like me as much anymore? But these are things that I would be thinking about during school, and like paying attention to how she was with, you know, another girl and is that going to be your new best friend? Or, you know, like, these are things that I would pay attention to. And I didn't even know why. And you know, I would go home and I would be crying if she couldn't spend the night and thinking that you know, that was the end of our friendship. And I just really wish I knew that she wasn't thinking the same thing. You know, like, she wasn't thinking that it meant that we weren't best friends anymore if she's hung out with someone else, but that's what I thought everything meant. So just the *idea* of social rejection. It didn't look like it looks for other kids. And I only know that now.

It's key to note that a ton of children, particularly during adolescence, experience social rejection and bullying, sometimes in severe ways. In fact, you might read this thinking that, since this is, technically, all in our heads, more attention should be paid to kids who are in active physical danger. And yes, please follow whatever training you've received on stopping bullying if you see it, but just because it's in our heads doesn't at all mean it isn't real – *I know that sounds like something from the final Harry Potter book but I would rather not quote that author* – and if it's affecting our performance in the classroom, then it matters all the same. It may seem minor from the outside, but it grows and expands in our brains until it takes over. "I've talked about it in therapy too," Rachel said, "that we remember the negative things much more than we remember all the other evidence that we have against the negative thing, so it magnifies."

And then, for most of us, it never really goes away. "Definitely was preoccupied with [social rejection]," Robyn said. "And hyperfocused on it. Observation of the details. You know, somebody raised their eyebrow a little bit when they responded and that, you know, that validated the story that I might have had in my head about that person accepting me or you know, being receptive to me or how I express myself. Yeah, it's something I probably still deal with a little bit . . . In retrospect, it is really silly. Yeah, it's really silly. Yeah, I got into a lot of colleges and I was a good enough student. I really thought I wasn't gonna get into college."

For my own part, I had done very well on those SATs I mentioned, and also on the subject-specific SAT II exams, but when I saw some of my classmates get rejected from top schools, I was convinced I wouldn't succeed in my own applications. Identity absolutely comes into play here, though, because my classmates, who were never all that mean to me despite tending to find me somewhat strange, started to take note of my race more explicitly in high school. I didn't hear any slurs or anything, but suddenly they "just wanted to ask me some questions" about affirmative action, and if I thought it was fair or not. But I guess that's a thing of the past now, right?

Still though, when I applied to an Ivy League university for early admission, largely on the advice of school leadership because I had zero confidence I'd get in, I was dreading the day that the letter showed up at my mother's house. When I opened it, and saw that it was large, a map of the school's town fell out of the package, and yet I still didn't want to believe I'd been accepted. All this time I'd spent convinced I couldn't measure up to my classmates and yet there I was, going to one of the top-rated schools around. But then I got there the following fall and immediately hyperfocused on being socially accepted again and my grades floundered until I found subjects I actually enjoyed. Funny how that works out.

Later, I tried to construct friend groups so that I had as low a chance of being rejected as possible, because it really did hurt me to open myself up and not be welcomed. I could not figure out what would work for people, but then, I also didn't really understand most people very well, so I was observing them like a nature documentary, taking mental notes and trying to present a reasonable facsimile of what I thought they liked. It didn't work very well, but I sure did keep trying and trying.

Marie told me of a similar process she followed and the frustration that followed not getting the results she expected:

> I had one incredibly great friend, and she was a church friend, so she wasn't at my school. And you know, she kind of gave me some talk like, 'You know, it's okay if people don't like you,' but to me, I wanted them so badly. I wanted them to like me because we were friends all of our lives. And to me, it was like all of a sudden, 'Why are you not my friend now? Like, what happened? Just because we're in middle school like you've decided to not like me. That's stupid.' You know, or at least I thought it was stupid. And so I think in terms of rejection sensitivity, and that perception of being rejected, it was always really difficult because I also kind of had this people pleasing tendency where it was like, 'Okay, I'm doing the things that I know you like, or I'm doing things with you that I know as far as we enjoy doing, yet you're still rejecting me.' So it was very frustrating and very angering, and I think I internalized a lot of that anger. Because whenever I'm in therapy, and we're like, talking about like, our inner child, our inner teen, my inner teen is very angry.

And I don't think I realized that until I got older, but I'm angry because a lot of these things never made any sense to me when it's like, 'okay, I'm checking your boxes.' Like I'm doing the things that you said would make me your friend and you're still not accepting me. I found it very frustrating because it was like, 'I'm doing the things that are being asked of me and I'm still being rejected.' And again back to this one really good friend kind of talking some sense into me where it was like, 'You're working so hard to please these people that don't care about you.' And to be told that at a young age, it's kind of like 'oh my god, like holy crap,' like that was a lot to take in at the time. But I look back and I'm grateful that she said that because I needed to hear it.

If you're not neurodivergent, we might seem like aliens, approaching social relationships like, as Marie says, boxes to check to receive approval. Especially given how many of the people I interviewed were classified as "gifted," have gone on to advanced degrees, or both, you might be thinking, 'how could we not understand that this isn't the way to build relationships?' But relationships are nuanced and messy, and, with rare exceptions, are not particularly predictable, so for most people, you treat people how you'd like to be treated and expect it will generate warmth. The problem for us is that the way *we*'d like to be treated is seen as unusual and sometimes off-putting, so we have to guess at how the rest of the world would like to be approached, and it's always pretty obvious that we don't actually know, especially as adolescents. I mentioned this way back in the communication chapter, but the way we show excitement and closeness often involves extensive monologues about whatever we're hyperfocusing on, and to us, if someone did the same, we might see that as love and affection. For a lot of others, though, this is rudeness, and so when our version of affection is rejected, we have no choice but to guess, mimic, and hope for the best.

At the school that I went to, a lot of the kids were, like I said, future celebrities or on that level of wealth. I won't pretend I grew up poor or anything, but whenever I actually socialized with these kids as I got older, it was clear that it was a whole 'nother level. I won't go too deep into the story, but when I finally got myself invited to a big party in 11th grade, I tried to do what everyone else was doing and ended up in a pretty dangerous situation which could have ended up a lot worse. When I got home, my grandmother, who was visiting for the weekend, told me I didn't have to do what everyone else was doing just to get them to accept me. She was right, but I sure didn't listen to her, at least not for way too long. I wish that I had.

Terry told me about the way they were singled out by their peers because of the unique way they processed the world and the many traits we've covered so far:

So, in America, there's something they call 'the dozens'[2] you're probably familiar with. And I don't like it. You know, other kids would do it to me, you know, and you're supposed to like laugh and come up with some witty thing but like, my brain doesn't work fast like that. And my brain perceives things very literally. And I didn't like it. And so the kids would make fun of me and I would cry. And after a while, they stopped trying to play with me. So the only time other kids engaged with me or had any kind of like social standing was when I was playing cricket, because I was really good. One thing I was really good at was hitting that ball. So when it came time to play Rounders, that's when I got picked first, but for every other thing you know, you have like a group in school. I'll always be picked last for any group because nobody wanted to be around me. They didn't particularly like me. And it got even worse when I was in high school because when I went to high school, none of the children from my primary school went to that high school. So I was starting all over again from scratch. And I was a weird kid, you know, I was a weird kid. I talked like a little adult, but, but I was still immature in ways that other kids picked up on and didn't like. So I ended up sort of like the leader of my own little merry band of misfits. And the four of us would hang out together at lunch. We would sing songs together. You know, we would talk about our pain, and we'd support each other emotionally. And we were the kids whose parents were very strict with us. And, and so our parents got to know each other over time. We were sort of allowed to sometimes go to each other's homes depending on where that home was. But for the most part, high school was very difficult for me. One year for Secret Santa, this girl wrote me this note basically saying, 'Sorry you had such a rough year this year and you have no friends and hopefully next year you'll have some friends,' you know, but that just never really manifested. And then when I was 16, I went over to the Boys School, which was next door because I was studying math and physics and they didn't offer math at the Girls School. And so the first year at the Boys School was great. You're one of four girls in your year and there's like 1100 boys in the school. You know, everything went pretty well. I sang in the prefects competition, and I won first place so that kind of added to my status. But then I wrote this very authentic article in the school annual magazine in which I basically explained to the girls that it wasn't all fun and games over at the boys school, that it's very difficult to be there. And particularly at the end of the day when you're trying to leave and you're surrounded by boys who have been hot in their classroom all day and they smell bad. And the boys did not like that I wrote this article. And so after that, they were really hostile to me. And I would do things I would be like walking down and they would call me names from like, along the hallway, that kind of thing. So, you know, just like being an authentic person who's not afraid to speak my mind in this very public way, meant that I really got ostracized by my peers.

I say again that the fact that many of us were bullied is not unique to neurodivergence or to being an NDSOC, but that so much of our social isolation was tied to our identities, and in ways that were often not said aloud, is what made our experiences what they were. Given how few of us are diagnosed, our classmates are unlikely to use ableist slurs against us, or at least not with the aim of doing so because of something they actually know about us. They mostly just think we're weird, and treat us accordingly, and if we bother to speak up for ourselves the way that Terry did, it can absolutely backfire, so our best hope is often to just wait until we can escape. And that's really not how school should be, especially given how many of us truly love to learn in our own neurodivergent ways.

Takeaways

I want to do something slightly different in this chapter. Some of the people you've already met did give out suggestions for how to support us in our rejection sensitivity and other related social issues, but most of that advice is similar to other takeaways you've already read. Suffice it to say, *check on the students you don't think you need to check on, and check on the ones who aren't necessarily giving you signals that they need to be checked on.*

But I have one more person to introduce you to, a fellow scholar I've worked with before who has written extensively about Disability Justice and Disability Studies in Education, and his name is, for the purposes of this book, Dr. Daniel Nava, who works at a university in the Midwest. He has a different perspective on the way that educators can be better prepared to support us, particularly with issues such as the ones described in this chapter. It's more academic than what you've read thus far, so I'll unpack it afterwards to bring this to a conclusion:

> At least in special ed, they call it differentiation. 'How do we differentiate the instruction to meet the needs of all our students,' but not in a color-evasive way, but in a way that can deconstruct the moment-to-moment interactions, that and in my work, you know, I call it critical emotional praxis, to critically think and feel before we interact with each individual student . . . There's really four models of disability, not just the medical or the social models of disability, but also the psycho-emotional disability as a

model and the intersectional disability as a model that accounts to what you were saying earlier. The social and gendered ways of the experience of being disabled as opposed to the impairment or, you know, the behavioral manifestations of what the storyline of the DSM is saying regarding the student as a label . . . And like, you know, they were labeling African-Americans 'maladjusted to society.' But we know nothing could be further from the truth. It's the counter narrative. It's actually how society you know, vis-a-vis the white gaze or other mechanisms of violence and control have historically, you know, shaped the ways in which are constrained the self and so, I think that's why it's so crucial, and I wouldn't be able to sleep at night if I put my teacher educator hat on if we are not orienting our teachers to the narratives of Black and brown and indigenous and youth of color kiddos at these intersections, so that they develop what I often say are the antennas that they need to have.

So there's a lot in there, and I shortened the response, too. What he's saying, as I understand it, is that disability in general, inclusive of neurodivergence, is inherently both a psycho-emotional and intersectional identity. That is, no one should be seen as "just" neurodivergent, and the internal experience you've now heard about for the last few chapters isn't just an additional factoid but is central to our identities. Teacher training programs have to better prepare new educators to be aware of this complexity, and since many don't do so, then the primary takeaway from this chapter, aside from checking in on us, is to *spend time and effort building up those "antennas" for what our experiences might be.* Part of the reason so much of this book is taken straight from my interviews is that I really wanted you to hear our authentic voices, so that when you have one of us in front of you – and you will – what Terry or Marie or Whitney said about their silent social isolation will keep ringing in your ears. You're already doing more than most by listening to all of our stories here, but you can talk to your colleagues about their own antennas and help your school build up the awareness it likely lacks. It'll be great if you can help support kids when they're in front of you, but if you can help their entire schooling experience transform into one where they don't feel rejected and don't have to hyperfocus on finding acceptance they inexplicably lack, then you'll have done an excellent job.

Notes

1 https://www.urmc.rochester.edu/behavioral-health-partners/bhp-blog/august-2023/rejection-sensitivity.aspx
2 From Wikipedia, for the unfamiliar: "The **Dozens** is a game played between two contestants in which the participants insult each other until one of them gives up. Common in African-American communities, the Dozens is almost exclusively played in front of an audience, who encourage the participants to reply with increasingly severe insults in order to heighten the tension and consequently make the contest more interesting to watch." Basically, it's a public diss battle.

12

Beating Ourselves Up
On the Corrosive Nature of Shame

This chapter is about the way that all of our experiences can add up to a destructive amount of toxic shame. Before I get into how that looked for us, though, it's important we have a clear understanding of what "shame" actually is; or, more accurately, the difference between "shame" and "guilt."

I'm about to quote another article from *ADDitude*, which is an online ADHD-focused magazine – *yes, I know the acronym doesn't match* – and I know that, to the persnickety academic sort with which I am very familiar, the fact that the data is focused on ADHD specifically and not neurodivergence in general will give some readers pause. But I've cited ADHD data, autism data, and all sorts of data here, because, since neurodivergence is not a medical diagnosis, there are few studies that center on the broader category, and even fewer on people of color as a subset. Besides, since so many of us have more than one flavor of neurodivergence, and since every flavor is itself a spectrum, the lines are so blurry as to be virtually nonexistent, and the stories will hopefully resonate regardless.

Anyway, evidence suggests that students with ADHD are given an astronomically large number of "corrective messages"

DOI: 10.4324/9781003465126-13

relative to their peers. As Dr. William Dobson notes, "For people with ADHD, shame arises from the repeated failure to meet expectations from parents, teachers, friends, bosses, and the world. It is estimated that those with ADHD receive 20,000 corrective or negative messages by age 10. They view themselves as fundamentally different and flawed. They are not like other people."[1] This excerpt begins to get at what I hope to convey in this chapter introduction, that for neurodivergent kids, it's more than simply having low self-esteem, which itself can be very damaging, but that we take our beliefs in our own inferiority and turn them back on ourselves. When you add the way we're classified as visible exceptions because of our identities, we experience even more pressure on a daily basis, and there's only so much a child or adolescent can take before we turn the disapproval we both receive and perceive into justification for self-hatred. It's not as simple as saying that we hate ourselves, which I wouldn't say is true of all of us, but more that we wish so much that the parts of us that made us easy targets would go away, and it's these very parts that represent the neurodivergence we should ultimately be proud of.

To return to the original point, as I understand it, guilt is feeling bad about something you believe that you did, whereas shame is feeling bad about who you are, and it's the latter that is all that much harder to break free from. We ought to be proud of what our brains are capable of, but because we are rarely in contexts that provide us with the support we deserve, we are likely to struggle through a swamp of shame that lasts until long after we're sitting in a classroom.

"People with ADHD who feel shame tend to withdraw into themselves – or hide behind a rage at the perceived source of the negativity," Dr. Dobson continued. "This may explain why people with ADHD fear letting others get to know them intimately or to see how they live. Individuals with ADHD harbor two horrible secrets: Their future is uncontrolled and uncontrollable and life can inflict wounding shame just as easily as it engenders success."

I honestly feel deeply fortunate that even this small number of people agreed to share their stories with me, because so few of us have ever truly been heard by the public. Many of us do "fear letting others get to know [us]," because our previous attempts have often been disastrous, but if it was as easy as choosing not to care about how we were perceived, it would be a pretty simple solution to our struggles. Unfortunately, we care when we're discarded, and it can really hold us back.

Counter-Narratives

The final enervating educational experience I'll share with you is about math research. Now, as I said a few times, I was really good at basic, nuts-and-bolts, arithmetic-based math, and struggled once I got into the more theoretical realm, but because I wanted to hold onto my identity as a Math Person, when I heard that a few of my "math friends" – *yes, I had "math friends"* – were enrolling in the math research class taught by Mr. Fiorentino, I jumped at the opportunity. Again, unlike some of the other teachers I've told you about, Mr. Fiorentino was kind to me – *he definitely got my name wrong when I saw him in my 30s, though* – even though he was clearly frustrated by my whole thing on occasion, and he helped me work my way through a very esoteric idea I had while basically not paying attention to what he was saying in class. The whole point of math research – a class that met *during lunch*, because you really had to be committed to it – was to submit to and prepare for a city-wide competition that was held every year, and the expectation was that every student in the class would not only apply but also that we would be accepted. Every single one of us did in fact apply and all but one of us was accepted, and so I had my very first chance to take part in a competition that was outside of my own school context.

There were three parts to this whole thing. In December, you'd present to the school, including a lot of the math teachers who were really just, and I say this with affection, overgrown nerds of the sort I would one day become who wanted to see what the kids had come up with, and then the larger competition was a few months later in March. I'd done well at the December presentation, my first time ever being "on stage," and then I was accepted into the March competition like most of my classmates. As ever, I didn't over-prepare, I just showed up ready to talk my way through my heavy, cardstock slides – *which my very proud father kept for more than a decade after the fact* – and I really impressed the judges. When they came back around to inform us who had been selected for the finals, they told me I'd done such a good job they had no notes for my presentation, just that I should probably pay more attention when other people were talking, which is funny.

Anyway, a few weeks later, I showed up ready to do the same presentation, and I guess I got harsher judges, because they had a lot of questions for me I wasn't prepared for, and they clearly weren't impressed by what I was trying to say. When the day ended, I got a bronze medal, whereas my two classmates got golds. In retrospect, my teachers should have done more than nothing to help me prepare, but I'm sure they figured I didn't need support, like they usually did.

Now, to be clear, by making it to the finals, I had achieved something worth putting on a college application, because very few kids made it that far every year, and everyone who made it to the finals got at least a bronze, but there was something about my friends "winning" that made it too much for me to bear. By this point, I'd come to believe I wouldn't achieve much academically, despite all evidence to the contrary, and because I, like Terry said in the last chapter, was the stereotypically "picked last" kid at most activities, I just wanted so much to win an award to feel better about myself that I made it about two feet out of the auditorium before I started crying. My father was confused, because I really had achieved something significant, and frankly I was confused too, but looking back, I was banking on each and every possible moment of glory as a respite from shame, and when these fulcrum points didn't go my way, I saw it as evidence I wasn't worth the pride my family had in me. And, as you've heard, plenty of my teachers didn't exactly help disabuse me of that notion when I refused to go along with their requests, and so it took until deep into adulthood for me to finally stop feeling the shame I'd developed in the classroom.

Similarly to my math research experience, an inner need to prove our perfection drove Marie to struggle with shame when she fell just short:

> I think the way shame mostly manifested for me was being super critical of myself, and being a performer. Like I could sing an entire song and it would be gorgeous. But if I had one note wrong, like I would just hyperfixate on how wrong that one note was and how I could have fixed it, how I could have done better. You know, I think a lot of it was I was never pleased. I never learned how to be okay with being good enough. Like it had to be perfect. And I think that is how shame manifested for me with this perfectionism. And I definitely noticed it, I think in terms of performing in terms of singing and all of that. Like, I remember one year I did a duet with a friend, and it was super fun. We had a great time singing it but instead of getting, like, the rating scale was like one is the best and five was the worst. *(What a bizarre scale!)* We got a two and I had never gotten a two at contests before and I remember being so upset about it because I was like, 'We deserved a one, it was so good, I can't believe he gave us a two.' Instead of celebrating the moment of like us having fun together singing and doing really well. Like a two isn't bad at all. I was so upset that it wasn't a one. You know, I was seeking perfection and I wasn't given perfection and that was disappointing. And I didn't know how to process that disappointment.

Speaking of perfection, I took Latin for several years, and one of the things Latin students do is take the National Latin Exam, which is a very private-school thing to engage in. Every year, after the tests were graded, they'd read out the awards people got for their performance. There were 40 questions, and once you got above about a 30, you'd be announced as having received a *cum laude* ("with praise") award. These are the same words that are appended to Bachelor's degrees, and I surely didn't get one then, but if there's an appropriate time to use pretentious Latin diction for academic performance, it's probably a Latin exam.

Anyway, every year, I'd get *summa cum laude* ("with highest praise"), which meant I'd gotten one or two questions wrong, and someone would get announced as having received *summa cum laude with a perfect score*, and I so desperately wanted it to be me. Having convinced myself that testing was my only academic value, it was moments like these I honed in on, but every year, I missed one or two, and got the penultimate award. One year, I didn't hear my name listed amongst the *summa cum laude* winners, and I figured that meant I was finally perfect, but then they just didn't call my name at all. Certain I'd gotten at the very least a *cum laude*, I approached the Latin teacher after the ceremony and asked if he could check again, which is a pretty whiny thing to do, but it turns out I actually had a point, because he found out that whatever organization ran the exam had straight up lost their copy of my test. He then graded it himself and told me I had, in fact, gotten 40/40, but because it wasn't officially recorded, it wouldn't count in their records. That's really just bad luck instead of mistreatment, but the way I attached potential public validation to this silly test meant that I was devastated.

I never really figured out how to just sit with my accomplishments, at least not until I got diagnosed and treated and came to accept myself. A clumsy, slow kid for most of my adolescence, I somehow transformed myself into an excellent marathoner in my late 20s, qualifying for Boston several times, including a six-week period in 2015 when I ran three marathons in a row. But I never allowed myself to enjoy it in the moment, because I'd set myself ambitious goals and then I'd let my doubts creep in during the race and fall short. I don't even think I ever let myself just enjoy an accomplishment without reservations until I got this last degree, and even now I still don't really believe it sometimes.

Marie added some vital perspective, though, explaining that all of this shame was internal – even if our schools didn't do enough to help us, it was our brains and our perceived distance from social norms that convinced us we'd never be good enough:

I'm from a single parent home. So when I talk about my home and I only talk about my mom, it's because she was the only parent figure. I don't think she necessarily put pressure on me. But she did expect a lot, like she expected me to perform. She expected me to try my hardest, but at the end of the day now that I've talked to her as an adult about things looking back, she genuinely didn't care that much. And I put a lot of that pressure on myself. Like most of it was internalized. And she just wanted me to be happy. And I thought you know, okay, I have all this pressure at school and at home, but there was no external force putting that pressure on me – it was myself. And it was because I knew that if I didn't perform a certain way, whether that means actually performing like singing or getting a good grade or having the right mannerisms or, you know, doing the right social script, whatever they were performing, if I wasn't performing, that I wasn't going to be good enough. And that is something that I internalized because of the shame that I felt growing up and I just, it never really clicked until I got a little bit older.

My parents certainly expected a lot out of me because they knew, correctly as it turns out, that I was capable. This is another place where being a neurological exception while also being a student of color comes in, because we were beacons of hope for our communities in a lot of ways, and we took that possibility and often floundered under its weight. I don't really blame anyone in my family for whatever was going on in my head, and it's why I'm writing this book for educators rather than parents. The only advice I'd give to parents of possibly neurodivergent students of color is to read through these chapters, see if you notice any patterns similar to your child, and talk to the school before the school has a chance to ignore their needs. These traits of ours, and particularly the emotional struggles, are not always seen as reflective of ADHD, autism, or other such conditions when exhibited by children of color, so, unfair though it may be, we're going to have to advocate for our own community, at least until more people tell these stories, as I hope they will.

"I have definitely dealt with a lot of shame," Ellie told me. "I feel like more shame came up for me once I had a diagnostic

label actually than before it but if I would get any negative feedback and it did come from teachers sometimes like, 'Whoa, why
are you so excited?' . . . It made me go into idle, withdrawn mode,
it would stick with me a lot and reverberate and yeah, I think
I have always had a strong sense of like, also, just shame to
having emotion, negative emotions, or problems."

I understand that allowing our fire to run free can lead to
a larger conflagration, so to speak, but since all of us have
experienced having water poured on our emotions, the deflation
that comes when we're invalidated like Ellie was can be excruci-
ating. I'm not surprised at some of our more dire statistics, particularly our overrepresentation among the prison population;[2]
if our internal dial is turned just a few more clicks in one direction, being diminished in this way could lead to really intense
external reactions, the type that leads to us getting punished and
derailing our academic trajectory in an irreversible way.

There's one more aspect of identity I want to bring up here
that I haven't touched on yet. Several of the people I interviewed
identify as biracial, including Robyn, Rose, and Whitney.
I mention this to say that, for them, it has sometimes created an
additional barrier to the perception of social acceptance, not so
much because I want to claim it's "harder" than being Black, but
just because finding your people is hard enough as an NDSOC,
and this added to their challenges.

"I think part of it, too, was that being biracial influenced a
lot of things," Whitney told me, to provide just one example.
"You know, I'm not white enough for the white kids and I'm
not Black enough for the Black kids. And so I always felt like in
the middle or othered in that way too. So that was also playing
in the back of my mind, right? Like not only did I feel different
and that affected my studying and my academics, but I also just
felt different based on my race, too. I really struggled with that
because my school was diverse, but like, again, we have all the
white kids in the white kid group and all the Black kids in the
Black kid group. And then I was kind of just stuck in the middle
and like trying to float or choose between those two as well."

Standing out can be a wonderful experience if you're in full
control of the ways in which you're different. You get a perfect

score on the Latin test? Great. You excel at sports? Awesome. But when what makes you different also makes it harder for people to embrace your full humanity, and there's really nothing you can do about these differences, you can end up wishing you were someone else entirely, and that's not an ideal way to go through your days in school. The only lesson I took from the shame I experienced, in that math research moment and otherwise, was to do whatever I possibly could never to admit how I felt, to shove it down so far I could try to forget about it.

Takeaways

"That's such a good question," Rachel replied when I asked what teachers could do to help us fight off our shame. "Like maybe if teachers asked more if you're doing okay. It would have been helpful, but I know that that's hard with class size and all this stuff. Like there's so many factors that make it hard for teachers to maybe even notice when one kid seems a little down."

It seems obvious, right? And I've already suggested it in the last chapter, checking on the students who don't necessarily set off alarm bells that they need help. So to a certain extent you already know what I'm going to say here. But ultimately, *if this emotional experience is about feeling bad not just about ourselves but about the parts of ourselves that make us stand out, then the way to counteract that is to put explicit emphasis on the inherent value of those sometimes-strange-seeming things that we do.* It's one thing for the way we do things to be tolerated so long as we get results and quite another for our unorthodox approach to learning to be held up as an example of innovation and creativity.

Whitney told me about one teacher of hers who was able to create an atmosphere that made the assignments feel secondary to her students' wellbeing. "I think she was able to use a lot of the same skills that she did as a social worker," she said. "And that, you know, made her a better teacher because she was really leading with compassion. Before we would even start talking about assignments for the day, I remember we would go around and just kind of share a little bit about our day or kind of what was going on and even if you were kind of making things up, she would pick up on those things. But I would just say like it was leading with compassion, right, like the assignments and the work, she definitely had us doing, but it always felt secondary in some ways. Just seeing us as people I think was her focus."

First of all, I know it's a lot to expect a working educator to attain the same skillset as a licensed social worker, and that not every social worker is inherently compassionate, but it's telling that that professional background helped this teacher align more effectively with students such as Whitney. Second, I know that the pressures of modern public education make placing students' humanity over their summative assessments nearly impossible, which a part of me believes is intentional on the part of the education instructional complex but we don't need to talk about that right now. Point being, *wherever you can take a moment to recognize a student's full humanity, particularly for students who stand out in ways they can't control, you might be making a bigger difference than you realize.* And if, like me, it would help you to systematize this process, you can make yourself a chart of students you've supported and rotate to ensure everyone feels seen.

Rose told me that she only felt full emotional support when she entered community college, which is fairly similar to Whitney's statement above about social work in that the educators in those contexts are expecting to interact with people from particular environments and, ideally, are positioned to support people who may have struggled in the past. "I felt inspired and more welcomed by a lot of the community college teachers I had," she explained. "And maybe that welcome was a bigger thing than I may realize, but I guess I just never really felt judged or rejected or weird in community college." The way I see it, an important lesson I've eventually learned both as a student and as an educator, and what I expect Rose experienced when she was placed in a different context, is that *taking the time to celebrate the seemingly small victories can have a big impact.* These days, I look for reasons to praise and encourage my students for things they probably wouldn't have expected to be noticed – a comment in a class forum, the lighting in a video they've submitted, and so forth – and these small wins can add up to major success in the long run. And again, be sure to celebrate these things in a way that assures students that what they might have felt judged or rejected for was a reason why they are being celebrated instead of an obstacle to overcome. Because we can't overcome our own brains – we can only hope to love them instead of being ashamed of the way they process the world. I think that with the many suggestions I've given so far, you will be better prepared to help us find that self-love we so dearly need.

Notes

1 https://www.additudemag.com/slideshows/adhd-and-shame/
2 https://www.ncbi.nlm.nih.gov/pmc/articles/PMC4301200/#:~:text=Overall%2C%20the%20estimated%20prevalence%20of,diagnoses%20compared%20with%20retrospective%20diagnoses

13

Outrunning the Pack
On the Ways We Can Excel When We're Supported

The final question I asked everyone was about their particular talents. Sometimes I phrased it as, "What are you better at than anyone else you know?" Regardless of the specific words I used, for some of the participants – though not all – I had to push them to brag a little. And yes, in this case, some of it should be considered bragging, but the problem with bragging is if it comes from a place where we lack any sense of humility whatsoever, not the mere act of celebrating an earned victory. Besides, I'd spent considerable time forcing them to wallow in traumatic experiences and I wanted the conversations to end on a positive note. So in this chapter, you're going to hear about our talents, the ones that may not have been recognized by our schools but which make us the exceptions we truly are.

Counter-Narratives

From Whitney:

> I'm thinking of it from my perception as an adult. I'm really good at operationalizing things, because I think

DOI: 10.4324/9781003465126-14

I struggled so much with like, understanding how to get from A to B. Like I have worked with organizations and come in and completely like created all the standard operating procedures for them so that they can, you know, function as a healthy entity. I'm also now really good at being in groups of people and like understanding a little bit of each person to then kind of be good at socializing. I'm really good at socializing when I need to be, if I'm not struggling anyways, that's besides the point. But yeah, I would say those are two things that I'm like, I'm really good at them. And I think a lot of it is because I want to like help people understand the ways that I could in the ways that I couldn't.

I told you that I really had to push people to brag on themselves, and you can see the hesitance Whitney spoke with in some of the words she chose. She hedges her bets – "if I'm not struggling anyways" – and I encourage any neurodivergent person reading this, despite what you've been told to believe about yourself, to walk and talk with the confidence of a mediocre neuromajoritized person. As has been said a few times in the book, this may scare or intimidate them, but if you can back up what you're saying – and I assure you, this is a very modest thing Whitney is saying here, since she really is great at creating processes – then after a certain point, they can't hold you back any longer.

From Rachel:

I don't want to sound like I needed to be complimented, but I needed the external validation of these teachers, like it really helped when they pointed out what I was good at. And so instead of pointing out, you know, like when you have progress reports for students, you know, even if a student is struggling in some way and maybe you want the student's parents to know that students see these progress reports, right, obviously, I think that there should always be one positive for any sort of perceived negative, because they need to know the things that they are good at. Because if you keep hearing that you're bad at these things, it really accumulates into this massive weight on your shoulders. So they are the ones like they told me that you're an out of the box thinker. They also said, you're really, really creative. The other ones that told me that and I believe them and I succeeded in these creative and out of box thinking, assignments, and so I knew I was good at that because they told me and I think that that was really helpful for me.

Again, it took a whole lot of self-negation to get to what she's really good at – thinking outside the box and creativity – and, as you may have noticed, there's a lot of "filler" words – *"like," "you know," that sort of thing* – in most of the transcript excerpts you've read, even the ones where I begged them to brag about themselves. In fact, and this will not surprise you, although I wanted the excerpts to remain authentic and to be sure I allowed their real voices to be heard, I'm sure you know that I edited out some repetition and some extraneous words to make it easier to read. If I let these excerpts be presented precisely as they truly were, the way I would have done so if this were more like my dissertation, there might have been "filler" language every fifth word. I'm not criticizing the people I spoke to – I speak the same way, you just get to "hear my voice" in entirely written language so, you know (*There's one!*) it's a little bit cleaned up. Suffice it to say, though I can't empirically prove it, I suspect that some of us have a tendency towards this because of our experiences being doubted and shamed for so long. Despite having more than two dozen degrees between all of us – *More than two per person!* – it really can be hard to speak with full-throated confidence when you weren't encouraged in doing so during your formative years.

From Marie:

What am I exceptional at? I think I'm an exceptional writer . . . I did take the writing test on the ACT and I got a 30. And then I remember when I did the GRE, which was awful and I scored terribly in the quantitative and the qualitative I did average in the verbal reasoning, but I got a 98th percentile for writing and I remember being like, 'Wow, this is confirmation that this thing I've believed all my life that I'm a good writer is true, because I wouldn't have scored this high if I wasn't a good writer.' And so I've always believed that I'm a good writer and I've always had people around me confirm that and that's been really reassuring. I'm also an exceptional singer and vocalist, and this was confirmed. You know, I discovered this at a young age although it was weird because in elementary school we would just have to take these like general music classes, and we would have them you know, every Tuesday or whatever day we had it. And it sucks because that teacher refused to recognize that I was a good singer. There was one other girl in the class that auditioned for our little local talent show. And he recognized her for auditioning, but not me. And I was like, 'What the heck man?' Like we both did the same audition. We both made it, which is great. We've made it through to like the actual show, but he recognized her for auditioning in the class but not me. And I remember being really like, I was probably in like, the third grade and I was offended because I was like, 'Okay, if we both went up there and sang, and you're proud of her for doing it, you should be just as proud of me.' So that's a moment of like, why is there this random hint of shame being dropped? But, you know, I always kept singing and I was one of the only kids at my school to make all-state and so that was like, confirming to me that like okay, all the hard work that I was putting in was being rewarded. And I like what you said earlier about, like competing with yourself. I think that's why I liked singing because it was a competition with me. Like I wasn't competing against anybody else. I was just competing against how good I could sing that day. And if I got there, then I got there and there were days that I didn't do well. Like there were days that I bombed my auditions and that happened and it sucked. But at the end of the day, it was a competition with myself. And I think that helps me view it. I don't know, I've never been a super competitive person. But competing with myself, I can do that. You know, because I can always show up and give my best that day. And if I don't show up and don't get my best, well, that's on me. Um, those are two things that I would say I'm specifically exceptional at writing and singing and then I think that's it.

While it was easier and quicker for her to pinpoint her talents, notice that there's still a story sandwiched in there about a time when these skills of hers were not appreciated. Each exceptional thing about us is tainted because of some experience, and there's always an underlying fear that what we believe about ourselves isn't really true. This is another reason that many of us point to our academic or standardized test performances when they're extremely strong, because there's that inner feeling of, 'You can't take this part away from me.' It's easy enough to say that exams are harmful, and that part of the education industry certainly is, but when we have few other directions to turn for the validation we're seeking, those round numbers are sitting right there.

Additionally, Marie's view on competition is interesting. Some would argue that the reason one should enjoy any sort of creative work, including singing, is just that it's meant to be valuable art, and that, unless you're on *The Voice* or up for a Grammy, you're not really supposed to be competing. But for us, whether we're running a marathon or singing, we often have to find some angle to use to push ourselves forward, and though it can still be fun when we succeed, it can also make the effort more joyless than it ought to be.

Rose, who had the most challenging educational trajectory of all of us, didn't feel she had a lot to share. She gave me a short list – "problem solving, analyzing data, finding patterns, being emotionally supportive" – but none of the full anecdotes others related. It can be very hard to let yourself love the things about you that others told you were a problem. So I'll just use this space to say, yes, all of those things, obviously, and that, considering what she did go through and the particularly challenging circumstances she's had to contend with, the fact that she's a bona fide credentialed scientist is nothing short of astounding. I refuse to put forth an "overcoming disability" narrative like others might, because the way her brain works, while an occasional impediment because of the way she wasn't supported, is precisely why she's made it through to where she is now. There is no Dr. Rose without her way of moving through the world, and that is absolutely true for all of us.

From Ellie:

> I think that the emotional things that could cause problems for me also are huge tools to social connection, like a very empathetic kid would want to help out my friends in any way I could, you know, really good at holding space for other people's emotions. Ironically, even if I would put mine on the backburner. I think that really, really strong drive for social connection has made me, you know, have a lot of relationships that ultimately are really beneficial for a kid to have like if you do get that one adult that does become invested in you. I think I have been able to like recruit people to you know, help me and work in my favor by being so kind of like earnestly curious and desiring that social connection so and like, feeling what other people are feeling a lot, like, kind of sometimes that can be a problem for me, but also I think it does really help with like empathy. And I think what's also come with that is a strong sense of justice. Like I mentioned before, thinking about what's right or what's fair or, I had so much social commentary for a young child that would just intuitively be like, 'That's not fair. Why is this person being treated differently?' and stuff and I think being an outsider, being neurodivergent and being in like a minority group gave me all those things that I think ultimately are strengths and make me a better adult, as well. And I always felt like I want to help people and I was, you know, a very, very prosocial kid, and I think that's cool.

It is! To be clear, when she says "prosocial," she doesn't so much mean wanting to socialize, though that seems to have been true of her; she's using it as the antonym to "anti-social," which in the clinical sense (that is, "antisocial personality disorder") means someone who is callous, corrupt, and cruel. The neurodivergent sense of justice recurs here, and she makes the important point that our additional wrinkle of being NDSOC means we inherently know what it's like to be singled out. Although, as she also says, we tend to do this at our own expense, we want others to feel comfortable and included, which are incredible emotional assets for a child to have, and even more important as an adult. This isn't to say we can't be cruel or lash out, as I am sure we all have, given how often we may have been in emotional pain – *not that that's an excuse, but it is an explanation* – but at our core, we are curious, and kind, and yearning for connection. And even if we don't always get it, we want others to have the chance at it anyway.

Robyn was as modest as Rose, which would be fairly galling if I told you her real name, since she's probably had the most professional success of all of us. This is not to say the rest of our careers don't matter, or that the only thing that matters is this version of achievement, but by all traditional metrics, she's an absolute superstar. All she said to me was, "I would say I'm pretty excellent at process improvement, making things more efficient. For that reason, I do consider myself to be a transformative leader. I'm excellent at running high performing teams. You know, motive, motivating teams, but also like executing efficiently." Although, short as her comment was, I guess it's pretty efficient, so, joke's on me I guess.

From Terry:

> I think I'm really good at reading people. I think that I know how to put people at ease, if I want to, if I so choose, when someone walks into the room. I have all this background and anthropology and psychology and sociology, as well as just like a lifetime of experience dealing with a lot of different people from different cultures. Not just all my international friends but also from

living in different cultures, first living in Trinidad, then in the US, also spending summers in Dublin, spending a semester in London, spending some time up in Belfast. I've been around a lot of different types of people. And I have long-term friend groups from different countries, including other European countries where I don't speak the language and so when someone walks into the room, I evaluate them both on a conscious and subconscious level. On the conscious level, there's things like, you know, I will immediately bring up difficult and complex topics. So that I can hear what their answers are, and I can see immediately, what are the things that they don't understand. As an example, I recently spoke to someone who's a Buddhist monk, and I said to her, 'Yeah, you know, like, I totally believe in the value of meditation, and I wish that I could meditate more. But you know, there's a difference between knowing the path and walking the path,' and instantly out of her mouth came, 'Yes, I tell people don't be lazy.' And the hair of my head just stood up on end because that tells me that she, number one, you know, today's enlightenment is tomorrow's ego trip and her ego trip is, 'I can meditate because I'm not lazy like those people over there who aren't lazy,' right? And two, she says that she tells that to people all the time, which means she blanket categorizes people as the only thing stopping them from meditating is laziness, which means she doesn't see her own privilege which means she doesn't see the complexity of people when she doesn't understand that laziness is a concept that is based in white supremacist, patriarchal culture and it's used to justify the exploitation of people and to make it their own fault when they can't do certain things, when she doesn't understand the concept of executive dysfunction, when she doesn't understand basic psychology. And once I know all of those things, then I can decide, 'Do I want to like lean into that and teach her through having conversation about all these things that she's missing out on? Or do I just leave her and disengage,' and my choice was the latter of the two. You know, she is who she is. And I don't need to be her teacher in the situation where she obviously thinks that she's the teacher.

Terry brought us all the way back to the lessons from the book's Introduction, tying together many of our chapters and the topics contained within them that exemplify our neurodivergences and how they're not flaws but simply differences and, if removed from the context of an exploitative system, might be positioned as strengths. This chapter, and in some ways this whole book, is about turning what are classified as our deficits into assets. They also pinpoint ways in which that sense of justice can be a true talent. Especially as someone who has chosen to write about racism and other forms of inequity, you really do have to know who is willing to learn before you bother wasting your time trying to improve everyone you meet. To be clear, I think anyone and everyone *could* learn why dismissing people as lazy is harmful and, ironically, is also intellectually lazy, and I would hope that certain chapters in this book might serve that purpose for readers, but not everyone really wants to learn, because oftentimes that entails admitting error, and humans are pretty bad at that. If you don't have the skills that Terry details here, you might spend years being friends with people who you think care about pushing for justice only to find out that deep down it was never a priority, and I've had to learn this lesson the hard way. These days, I give everyone two chances, since I'm a teacher with expertise on the subject, and if they show a genuine curiosity and openness by my second attempt, then we've got an opportunity. After that, well, as Terry says, they are who they are, and I'll leave my lessons to my writing and hope they read it someday.

Aside from things you've heard me say already about being good at testing, which is mostly just a combination of long-term memory and pattern recognition, and also the fact that, as my confidence grew in adulthood, I found more and more ways to tap into my hyperfocus almost at will – the skill being tapping into it, the hyperfocus itself being a trait I happen to have – I'm a really good teacher. Maybe it's because, like Ellie said, I remember all these stories I've shared about the ones who just thought I was a nuisance or, at best, a talented kid who disappointed them, but I can stand in front of a room, I can command attention, and I can help learners reach their goals.

I didn't know a single thing about teaching when I started my career. It happened on a lark and a desire to go to parties and see new countries. My first year, I was pretty bad at it, like a lot of rookies, and I was convinced that, after my contract ended, I'd go home and try and find something else to do. A lot of the people who go and teach overseas either just stay abroad forever or they come home and realize their foreign teaching experience doesn't count for a lot and they struggle to figure out a path – it's happened to a good number of the people I met in Korea. But after the financial crisis hit in late 2008, going home seemed unwise, yet another year just struggling through work was both unpleasant and boring, so I wanted to get good at it.

I still knew nothing of pedagogy, mind you. But I had one student who spent every class goofing off and making noise while I was talking. Male teachers tend to wear suits in South Korea and my school refused to keep the AC on during the summer – *the school year runs March to December* – so I was just melting into a puddle every day, and here's this kid just being . . . annoying. At first I was mad, because, with the sensory issues I didn't realize I had, I was so physically uncomfortable I couldn't keep the classroom together. But one afternoon I noticed he actually looked despondent and I asked him what the problem was. He told me that my English class was just too easy for him. He was bored.

That may seem obvious to you if you're an experienced teacher, but I wasn't, and I had yet to come anywhere close to a diagnosis or a real understanding of myself. All I knew was that I understood how he felt, and a part of me thought, if I can find a way to bring the light out of this kid, I can probably do that for anyone. I had no control over the legitimately beginner-level material, as many of you probably have little control over system mandates, but I got that kid on my side by giving him Black history figures to research. He'd come to my office to ask me questions about the people he read about, and even though the class was still way too easy for him, he participated in the exercises and helped out the students who were struggling.

To this day, I think I have two jobs in a classroom. Either I need to help the people in front of me to find out what's exceptional about them, or, if they already know, I just need to clear the tracks so they can start moving as fast as they want to. By now all of my students are young adults or older, but I've taught ages six (*a summer program in Korea*) to 86 (*computer classes at a senior center*), and all I want to do is make sure they never feel the way I once did. If I can do that, I can help them learn. And so can you.

Takeaways

You may not have full control over your material, but, as many of us have said, we do need ways to know we're great, because we've probably received the message that we're not. It's one thing to generally praise our unorthodox way of thinking, communicating, writing, feeling, and learning, it's another to actually give us credit for it. So *if there's any way to give out extra credit for coloring outside the lines, or coming up with an answer you may not have expected, or approaching an assignment in an innovative way, add it to the rubric.* Let us know that the way we are is *why* we're great, and not just something we need to overcome. Because, as I've said a million times by now, we can't overcome our own brains, and we shouldn't have to try. We're great as we are, and it's time that that was recognized.

Conclusion

A Word about IEPs

I said I would come back around to the topic!

Now, I could give you a massive meta-analysis of the impact of IEPs and the language within them on neurodivergent students, but you're only going to end up with the same idea I mentioned however many pages ago, that kids of color are overindexed into special education despite being underdiagnosed with conditions that fall under the neurodivergence umbrella. To be clear, there is nothing wrong with having traits that would be best served via special education, and some neurodivergent students of color are appropriately placed there – *even if the chances they're treated fairly within that system are low* – but, although there is obviously some overlap, "special education" and "neurodivergence" are hardly the same thing. Of course, for the many NDSOC who aren't diagnosed as children, like almost everyone in this book, there likely won't be any IEP to work from in the first place.

Nevertheless, you may come across a student that you suspect would fit alongside the people whose stories you've heard

DOI: 10.4324/9781003465126-15

here who happens to also have an IEP, be it for a neurodivergent condition or some other reason, and I can't tell you to just ignore the law. What I want to do briefly, then, is take a glance at what an IEP might look like through the lens of our experiences and provide suggestions accordingly.

There are plenty of examples of sample IEPs around the internet, but a pretty standard one can be found on the website of the National Association for Special Education Teachers, and I think you'll shortly see what I mean when I say that what's presented as supportive falls quite short of what our community needs, particularly for NDSOC.

This example IEP[1] includes the following goals:

1. _____ will develop social understanding skills as measured by the benchmarks listed below.

   a. _____ will raise their hand and wait to be called on before talking aloud in group settings 4/5 opportunities to do so.

   b. _____ will work cooperatively with peers in small group settings (i.e., share materials, allow peers to share different thoughts) 4/5 opportunities to do so.

   c. _____ will develop an understanding of the relationship between his/her verbalizations and actions/effect on others 4/5 opportunities to do so.

   d. _____ will engage in appropriate cooperative social play interactions initiated by others 4/5 opportunities to do so.

   e. _____ will engage in cooperative social play interactions by allowing others to make changes or alter the play routine 4/5 opportunities to do so.

   f. _____ will engage in appropriate turn-taking skills by attending to peer's turn and waiting for own turn 4/5 opportunities to do so.

   g. _____ will appropriately acknowledge an interaction initiated by others by giving an appropriate response, either verbal or non-verbal.

   h. _____ will develop an understanding of the rationale for various social skills by stating the reason when asked (i.e., Why do we say excuse me?)

i. _____ will increase social awareness of environment by stating what is taking place in environment or imitating actions of others 4/5 opportunities to do so.

j. _____ will increase safety awareness by stating the effect of various situations 4/5 opportunities to do so.

k. _____ will identify appropriate social rules and codes of conduct for various social situations 4/5 opportunities to do so.

l. _____ will refrain from interrupting others by exhibiting appropriate social interaction skills 4/5 opportunities.

There's obviously more to it than that, and the organization does make clear that this is just an example and can/should be modified, but if you've read all the way through this book, I think you can see how this language is stigmatizing, and, in the wrong hands, could be particularly dangerous for students like us.

First of all, throughout, there is an assumption that "appropriateness" is an objective standard, whereas you've read about how we process the world and communicate differently from others no matter how hard we attempt not to. Second, the direct reference to talking out of turn – several times, in fact – means that any and all of us could have failed to meet these standards. And third, most sadly, the students in question are being measured explicitly on how well they "[imitate] actions of others." As you know by now, most of us try desperately to mimic our classmates, but it only leaves us looking even more different and further isolates us from our peer group.

There are IEPs out there with less stigmatizing language, but let's say you're presented with this one, or something similar, or whatever level of detail your local and state policies provide. What can you even do?

I wonder if you can tell what I'm going to suggest based on what everyone in this book has said, but, basically: *make it a game*.

If you've got a student of color who talks out of turn, or exhibits however many of the traits you know now of, and you need to measure them against benchmarks such as these, make it fun for them. They have to learn how to mimic their classmates?

Include an activity where everyone practices copying each other. They have to avoid blurting things out? Tell them to write it down and/or speak with them to see if they can become *the best* at biting their tongue, and then be sure to give them explicit credit for doing so at the end of class. This all depends on what's written, of course, but the point is not to punish them for their brains, and to make use of their skills to achieve a mandated set of goals, which will help them flourish once they're away from the supportive classroom you're sure to provide, as well as preventing them from feeling the shame that many of us did.

This is but one set of examples, but this is how I think you can contend with IEPs in an affirming but effective way.

On the Importance of Fostering Solidarity for NDSOC

Unless you have the same set of intersectional identities as we do – and maybe you do and that's why you're reading – there's ultimately only so much you can do from the outside. Create the best environment that you can, but that's just one part of the battle, and without a community around us in the school, we still may end up yearning for closer peer relationships like many of us did. If you read through all of this and start to notice these traits in a few of your students, not only might the earlier suggestions help you decide to bring similar students together, but also, you can talk to your colleagues about the kids in your classrooms and listen to learn who around the school might be having these experiences. Maybe there's an opportunity for a club or an informal group to be created and supported by admin-istration, even for kids who have no formal diagnosis. Or maybe it's just something you can tell your school to bring in speakers to discuss, rare though we are in the public sphere. Anything you can offer to help us find our way to the solidarity we often lack would be crucial for our healthy development.

When we're isolated, we don't even recognize when we might share traits with someone else. I remember, early in high school, a parent of an older classmate called my dad's apartment to ask him if I'd ever been singled out in ways that her son had.

Her son was known for making unusual gestures and noises in class, and we used to argue about subways and geography and other ephemera because we lived near each other in Brooklyn. In retrospect, diagnosis or not, we were cut from similar cloths, and he was getting a lot of the same in-class treatment from his teachers that I was. His mother knew that simply telling the "progressive" school that singling out her son was racist wouldn't get her very far, not in a pre-Black Lives Matter era anyway, so she wanted to see if another student could back him up.

So my dad asked me if I thought anything like this had ever happened to me. At the time, I honestly never even spent time worrying about all the stories I've written about here. Not Mr. O'Donnell, not Mr. Rossi, not Mr. Christopher, none of it. I wouldn't say I "blocked it out" and had the memory recovered later, more that I was so concerned with my social standing that I was always trying to think of some new tactic to connect with my peers. I only had the clarity to consider that I'd been treated differently from my classmates after a lot of maturity, treatment, and (relative) mental stability, and only once I started doing the research that eventually led to my diagnosis did I contextualize the fact that my identities were being denigrated, even without the use of any slurs. All of this is to say that my understanding of racism in my early teens was basically just Jim Crow and earlier, and since I knew nothing like that had ever happened to me, I told my dad as much. My dad trusted my account, and as far as I understood it I was fully telling the truth, and so my friend's mom was left to fight for her son without the solidarity he should have had. He ended up okay, far as I can tell – we're still acquaintances. But, from conversations we've had as adults, he certainly gained a visceral understanding of racism much earlier than I did.

I let my classmate down because I couldn't recognize our similarities. I let him flounder because I was trying so hard to mimic everyone else that I figured anyone being singled out deserved it, myself included. If I'd had a group, or a club, the younger me might not have joined, but maybe if you tried to put one together now and invited people, listing some of our traits positively and with warmth, maybe some NDSOC would check it out and find themselves a home they didn't know they needed. It's worth a try.

Where Should Research Go from Here?

Part of the reason I did all this was of course because, as they tell you when you start a doctoral program, there is a gap in the research I thought I could start to fill. I've made a side career out of finding niches that are underexplored, first writing about white supremacy in language education and now collecting these stories and sharing them with you. My hope is that this has a similar trajectory to a couple of my academic articles, and more people take up the mantle to bring these counter-narratives to the eyes and ears of people who need them.

I'm endlessly skeptical about the value of quantitative studies when they're done via traditional methods. Or, I should say, skeptical about their value in terms of achieving social justice on their own. I am of the belief that there's no one who doesn't care about us that is suddenly going to change their entire mindset solely because they read that ADHD/prison population estimate cited in a previous chapter. This book, and all of my work, is qualitative in nature, and narrative-based in format, because I believe that stories are what move the world, for better or worse. However, unless some powerful figure is deeply inspired by our stories here and decides to rip up a local statute and start from scratch, stories alone aren't going to change policy, and for lasting change, codified policy is needed. So, we're going to need some numbers. But what numbers should be sought?

Well, first, we really don't know how many of us are out there. You could attempt a massive survey of teachers or parents regarding their children, but given our rates of diagnosis it would only be a broad estimate, like every statistic describing us thus far. If you tried to put together a study within a school system, you would run into problems passing through an Institutional Review Board if your criteria didn't require formal diagnosis, so we're back with the same set of issues. My best idea would be to start with a list of traits such as the ones that are covered in the previous chapters – and even a few more – and then do some purposeful sampling of adults of color across a given geographic area, asking them to say yes or no to whether or not they matched the criteria. You could follow that up with extensive interviews of whoever responded and was interested, so you'd gradually end up with a large database with which you could better estimate how many of us are out there, and then, importantly, how many of us would never have thought that their sensitivity to light might have something to do with neurodivergence.

I'd also want to know if my assumption that our outcomes are pretty binary – extraordinary or terrible – is correct. I'm sure there's something of a spectrum, but I do wonder if there's as stark a divide between our successes and our struggles. Surely all of that would be impacted by other axes of oppression, but you could control for that and focus on neurodivergence and race.

What we really need, though, is a far greater understanding of the emotional aspects of neurodivergence, both in general and in particular as they intersect with racism. There's enough of a body of research demonstrating the trauma that systemic racism causes, but what does neuronormativity when combined with racism lead to, psychologically and physically? And what methods can be developed to address these intersectional challenges? Of all the professionals I've seen who helped me with whatever's been going on in my head, finding one who listed specialties in both neurodivergence and racism has been impossible – I just had to find one of the former who happens to be Black. Our stories here aren't all the same, but there are enough threads that could be picked up and explored by anyone who wants to know about us. It's one thing for people who read this book to take these lessons into their classrooms as I hope that they do. But all the other adults like us, especially the ones still unsure of why they don't quite connect with the world around them, deserve to be advocated for all the same. So I hope these messages reverberate strongly enough that we can be taken care of too.

Final Guidance from the Experts

You could consult a doctor about how to treat us. You could ask a fellow teacher what they've done when they've taught one of us. But the real experts on what would have helped us as neurodivergent students of color are the NDSOC themselves. So I wanted to leave you with their best pieces of advice for teachers, and this is some of what they told me.

Whitney: Help us find the tools

> I did have one teacher, Ms. Kim, who would pull me aside and, you know, I think really helped me understand that there were tools I wasn't using that I could use to be more successful . . . For me personally, just guidance, right? Having someone pull you aside and being like, you know, 'here are ways to direct my attention to other things,' that would have been helpful, right. Like, for instance with Ms. Kim, she would you know, give me other little assignments or other little things to work on and like, just having someone do that like that felt like I was seen even though it wasn't even that big of a gesture in a lot of ways, but like giving me some other outlets besides just the assignments and extracurriculars. For me, that would have been helpful, having some other things to direct my attention to because that then helped me focus on the material in the classroom, because I had other things to work on or other, you know, things to look forward to. Like, 'Oh, Ms. Kim needs me to come help with grading papers or to come help sort the room' or whatever. Those other little things like helped me then focus on what I needed to do in the classroom and also made me feel supported just as a person.

Rachel: Validate, validate, validate

> I would say, validate it, and not be like, 'Oh, don't feel that way.' Just be like, 'I understand that you're feeling this

way and that's okay.' I think that would have been really helpful. Instead of the messages that I got a lot, which were 'Oh, don't feel that way there.' You know, 'there's no reason to feel that way.' Because then that invalidates your whole experience. And that's not a good thing. So just validating experiences, I think would be really helpful. And I don't know how you do that, if you have more training on socioemotional things for teachers, but I know there's something I learned in therapy is that just validating and acknowledging is really, really important . . . I think that's why it's so important to validate instead of saying, 'Oh, you shouldn't feel that way.' Because it's like, 'Wait, do you know that the whole world is trying to make me feel this way?' Because, like, you know, I go through the world differently than you do. So I think that's why it's so important that teachers don't say things that invalidate the experience or like don't try to cheer us up.

Marie: Check in with the kids who claim not to care

It got to the point where I kind of went through this sort of transformation from like, I'm people pleasing so hard to I kind of didn't give a crap at all. I'm like, 'I don't care if they like me.' Like I went from one extreme to the other very quickly, where it was like, I'm gonna do everything I can to try and be friends with these people to where it's like, 'I don't care if you like me at all.' And so I think that it's funny because I was voted most outspoken in high school, and I'll never forget, of all people who could say this, it was my cousin. She said she did not want to be voted most outspoken because she didn't want people to view her as a bitch. And she said that to my face after I was voted most outspoken and I was like, but I really didn't care if she saw me as bitch. I was like, 'I am who I am. And I don't need your opinion to validate me.' So I've kind of gone through the spectrums of, 'I'm hurt, nobody wants to be my friend,' and internalizing all of that to the other end of where I don't give a f what you think about me, you know.

Daniel: Center the emotionality of disability

I would say we need a new model of disability. Because the model of disability is to other and to pathologize. That emotion. You know, other historians have called it 'the hunt for disability' and to sit with a child or someone's experience of disability. It's really important to what, how, and why we do what we do in schools. And lately I've been thinking about this because I've been doing a lot of writing at these intersections. And that's why we, in the culture, we kind of just have two models of disability operating, the medical or the social model . . . It's an intersectional experience. It's not that it's a purely singular vector, you know, and just the whole idea that emotions, feelings, and aspects are social as opposed to purely biological, or, you know, individual. I think teachers need to know that, too . . . And sometimes we experience emotionally and viscerally all these institutional policies and practices or classrooms? You know? It's not until we give ourselves the space and grace to reflect on those experiences that we're able to process in a sense.

Rose: Build relationships with those who don't demand attention

There's a tendency to overvalue extraversion and that can lead to teachers not building relationships with their more introverted students or assuming that because they're still that there's no problem. And, you know, you're still, and if the work looks okay, and everything's fine, but a lack of engagement in class. I think that at any age, if someone who's just always quiet, typically not engaging, there's an opportunity to help that person develop and open up and contribute. [Help] the kid figure out how, or maybe they have issues with the timing of speech or they're being bullied or things like that. I don't think it should be as acceptable as it is, the person in the back that's just quiet to be completely ignored and to disengage. But that's not success as a teacher to me. You've spent most of your energy paying attention to the loudest people in the room instead of just assuming that the quiet person is fine . . . And I think that that's a problematic way of thinking. Yeah, it's obviously biased by my introversion. I find it just in general, like all the things we were talking about with learning styles and communicating style, like everything defaults to the outgoing, extraverted person's way of doing things. That is often what I found to be the case in jobs in business and academia. On the other hand, I feel like I try to understand everybody, like everybody has strengths and weaknesses.

Ellie: Proactively seek out psychological and neurodivergence education

You're not going to have diagnoses [for these kids] and at the same time, you can just know that statistically, some number of your students are going to have a neurodivergence. I feel like [psychological] education around emotions, I think could be so helpful too. I also feel like neurodiversity education as well; it might be a topic that comes up now but not when I was going to school, you know.

Robyn: Be adaptive in creating supportive spaces

So I think you have to almost act as if like, rather than, rather than assuming students can self identify and can articulate their own needs and their accommodations that they may need. I think there may have to be some assumption that you have some of these students in your classroom, setting up situations, I mean, setting up quiet work areas as much as possible I don't think harms anyone, and may benefit everyone slightly in their own ways, just as an example. Figuring out ways that you can make a space safe or supportive for students, if they're experiencing some of these challenges, whether they are known to you or whether or not they are able to communicate. You know, I think being adaptive in teaching style is really helpful in this manner with this issue.

Terry: Recognize flashes of brilliance wherever and whenever they may occur, challenge your colleagues to do the same, and protect your students from the people who won't support them

I think that teachers themselves need therapy and they need to up their emotional intelligence. I think that teachers need to pay attention to the other teachers around them and how they are treating and talking to students. I think that when a child is showing extreme, like showing hyper focus in certain areas, for instance, when I was a child, I wrote a short play, and I gave it to my English teacher and asked her to read it, and she didn't read it and didn't give it back to me. And if she didn't feel like she had the time to do it, she shouldn't have taken my work from me. I feel like there were a lot of bad actors among my teachers. And I don't know how you really work on that other than to pay attention to how other teachers are talking about their students. Because what I have found is that as you know, as a person who has spoken to other faculty members about their students, you start to notice when there are faculty members that say things like, 'You know, I've never had a Black student who has gotten an A in my class.' You know, when faculty members say things like that, they need to be called out. They need to be called out, they need to be coached, they need to be corrected, and I don't know that you can protect an individual child from bad actors who are other teachers other than by paying attention to the teachers, as well as the students. I don't think that there's anything teachers can really do to step into children's social groups, you know, like, what did I really need? You know, could someone have stepped in and been like, 'Hey, you communicate differently from other people. Let's talk about how to handle it when other students are trying to challenge you. They're really just making a joke.' And, you know, like, I don't know how you coach a child who is sensitive and doesn't want to engage in "the dozens" with other children. How do you coach that child in dealing with it when other people are teasing them? And it's supposed to be funny and socially acceptable? You know, do you tell the whole class that not everybody wants to engage in that behavior and that you need to get consent before you do that. Maybe [social] consent practice is really the issue, getting other students in the class to be more aware of the fact that people will think differently and have different needs. And, you know, maybe creating situations where I could thrive without having support from people who didn't give me support . . . It was upon graduation from the Girls School, that everybody in the school all of a sudden figured out that I was brilliant, that I was at the top of my class because I graduated, and I got this prize, but then all the girls who were mean to me, all of a sudden wanted to be my friend, but I was gone. So all of my brilliance that could have created an opportunity for other girls to see me and want to be friends with me was completely wasted in terms of social cachet because it didn't come until the final day.

Justin: Please be patient with us

I know we can be frustrating. We might get on your last nerve. And sometimes we come off as so inherently cap-able that when we don't seem to be able to get anything done, it just doesn't make any sense. But trust me, we still need you to be gentle with us and help guide us to the paths that will keep us moving forward. Everyone in this book figured things out eventually, and when we neurodivergent students of color find out what we're good at, we can do amazing things. But there's no such thing as a child that doesn't need love and respect from their teachers, even the ones who seem like they don't need any support at all. I ask of you, readers, not to give up on the kids in your classroom who think, act, *and* look like us. There's nothing to be done to protect the children we once were from a world that isn't all that friendly to the way we move through it, but you can protect the ones in front of you right now, and all the neurodivergent students of color you meet in the future.

Just try not to tell them they're annoying, okay?

Note

1   https://www.naset.org/fileadmin/user_upload/Autism_Series/Examples_IEP_Goals_Objectives_for_ASD.pdf

Acknowledgments

First things first, to the people and other beings that live with me: There's no way I'd be able to do any of this, both practically in terms of time commitment, and emotionally in terms of support and an unwavering belief in my ability, without my wife, Alissa. The person who is always happiest to see me is still my son, Ezel, and maybe he'll be able to read all this pretty soon, though I'm sure he'll find it boring. And, he definitely won't be able to read this, but Neptune, my Lagotto Romagnolo, always loves me, depending on whether or not I have treats, which is a pretty fair exchange.

To my family, blood, step-, and -in-law, and my parents in particular, you all did what you have always done and have given me the love I may not have always received from others at my institutions, and it's how I persevered one way or another. I'm sure this was occasionally uncomfortable to read for you, but know that it'll do a lot for the kids like me in the future.

I have to thank the team at Routledge who supported and collaborated with me in this production, in particular Lauren Davis, Hannah Sroka, Charlene Price, and Sarah Pearsall.

Thank you to Cheryl Matias and Paul Gorski, for selecting a chapter of mine for an edited volume and telling me they wanted to include me not just because of what I wrote but also because of how I wrote it, a theme that obviously recurred throughout this book. And a double thanks to Paul for working with me on coming up with the right idea to pitch to Routledge years later.

I am grateful for all the scholars whose work has inspired me and pushed me to be critical of systems while retaining hope that equity is possible. I'm cynical, but I refuse to be pessimistic, if you understand the difference, because if folks like me give up, then who's going to be left to fight?

To my classmates in my doctoral program, the first group of academic peers who really accepted me and made me feel like

I wasn't a nuisance to learn with, that embrace played a larger part than you know in helping this book get made.

To my erstwhile supporters from the language part of my scholarship, I can never forget you, because it's how I learned to challenge conventions in the education world and where I got my start shaking my fist at clouds. So, Lesley, Gabriel, Scott, even when I don't write about language, your support is in the work.

To the various mentors and supporters I've had in my scholarship on race and disability, including David Hernández-Saca, David Connor, and of course Catherine Voulgarides, this was a realm I never would have thought to enter, and if it weren't for all of you and others, I'd still be writing two-page articles about language.

To the many neurodivergent people I've formed bonds with over the last five years, near, far, of all races but particularly people of color, sometimes it can feel like we're all we've got, but I hope that this effort can make you all feel like there are people out there who understand your experiences.

To the real life versions of Whitney, Rachel, Marie, Daniel, Rose, Ellie, Robyn, and Terry, thank you for trusting me with your stories, your insights, and your authenticity, because, with no exaggeration necessary, I couldn't have done this without your participation and trust.

To Mr. O'Donnell, Mr. Rossi, Mr. Christopher, and all the teachers I came across who left me to flounder . . . to paraphrase the great poet, Montero Lamar Hill, *y'all was never rooting for me anyway*.

But to all the other teachers, the ones that didn't make their way into a negative anecdote, the ones who saw what value I had and nurtured it until I blossomed into an educator myself, you're the reason this book can exist, because I wouldn't have written it if I didn't believe wholeheartedly that everyone reading it had the capacity to do for their students what you all did for me. In particular, all of my English teachers and professors, who saw I had something in me long before I saw it in myself, and kept pushing me to write even when I didn't want to. The list is long but I'll single out Alex Darrow, who encountered me when I spent more time coming up with lies and excuses for why I wouldn't just do my homework in seventh grade, and then again when I was pounding out 200-page screenplays for no good reason in 12th, and of course, Jane Avrich, who saw me before I learned how to hyperfocus – in fourth, fifth, and sixth grade – while I was sort of figuring it out – in ninth – and then when I knew how to get the words out, in 12th. Whenever I read through my work and find myself liking it, I'm always making a little green left-handed checkmark in my head.

And to all of you reading this, thanks for giving my work a shot. I hope it was worth your time.